W9-AQS-054

Current
CONTROVERSIES

Drug Legalization

Other Books in the Current Controversies Series

Current
CONTROVERSIES

Drug Legalization

Noël Merino, Book Editor

GREENHAVEN PRESS
A part of Gale, Cengage Learning

GALE
CENGAGE Learning

Detroit • New York • San Francisco • New Haven, Conn • Waterville, Maine • London

GALE
CENGAGE Learning™

Christine Nasso, *Publisher*
Elizabeth Des Chenes, *Managing Editor*

© 2011 Greenhaven Press, a part of Gale, Cengage Learning

Gale and Greenhaven Press are registered trademarks used herein under license.

For more information, contact:
Greenhaven Press
27500 Drake Rd.
Farmington Hills, MI 48331-3535
Or you can visit our Internet site at gale.cengage.com

For product information and technology assistance, contact us at

Gale Customer Support, 1-800-877-4253
For permission to use material from this text or product, submit all requests online at www.cengage.com/permissions

Further permissions questions can be emailed to permissionrequest@cengage.com

Articles in Greenhaven Press anthologies are often edited for length to meet page requirements. In addition, original titles of these works are changed to clearly present the main thesis and to explicitly indicate the author's opinion. Every effort is made to ensure that Greenhaven Press accurately reflects the original intent of the authors. Every effort has been made to trace the owners of copyrighted material.

Cover image © Joseph Sohm/Visions of America/Encylopedia/Corbis.

LIBRARY OF CONGRESS CATALOGING-IN-PUBLICATION DATA

Drug legalization / Noël Merino, book editor.
   p. cm. -- (Current controversies)
   Includes bibliographical references and index.
   ISBN 978-0-7377-5097-3 (hardcover) -- ISBN 978-0-7377-5098-0 (pbk.)
   1. Drug legalization--United States--Juvenile literature. 2. Drug control--United States--Juvenile literature. I. Merino, Noël.
   HV5825.D77667 2010
   363.450973--dc22
                                                    2010019299

Printed in the United States of America
2 3 4 5 6   15 14 13 12 11

ED174

Contents

Chapter 2: Should U.S. Drug Policy Be Reformed?

Yes: U.S. Drug Policy Should Be Reformed

Chapter 3: Should Marijuana Laws Be Relaxed?

Crude marijuana, in smoked form, is not recognized as a safe, effective medical treatment and should not be legalized for medical use because better alternatives exist.

Foreword

By definition, controversies are "discussions of questions in which opposing opinions clash" (*Webster's Twentieth Century Dictionary Unabridged*). Few would deny that controversies are a pervasive part of the human condition and exist on virtually every level of human enterprise. Controversies transpire between individuals and among groups, within nations and between nations. Controversies supply the grist necessary for progress by providing challenges and challengers to the status quo. They also create atmospheres where strife and warfare can flourish. A world without controversies would be a peaceful world; but it also would be, by and large, static and prosaic.

The Series' Purpose

The purpose of the *Current Controversies* series is to explore many of the social, political, and economic controversies dominating the national and international scenes today. Titles selected for inclusion in the series are highly focused and specific. For example, from the larger category of criminal justice, *Current Controversies* deals with specific topics such as police brutality, gun control, white collar crime, and others. The debates in *Current Controversies* also are presented in a useful, timeless fashion. Articles and book excerpts included in each title are selected if they contribute valuable, long-range ideas to the overall debate. And wherever possible, current information is enhanced with historical documents and other relevant materials. Thus, while individual titles are current in focus, every effort is made to ensure that they will not become quickly outdated. Books in the *Current Controversies* series will remain important resources for librarians, teachers, and students for many years.

In addition to keeping the titles focused and specific, great care is taken in the editorial format of each book in the series. Book introductions and chapter prefaces are offered to pro- vide background material for readers. Chapters are organized around several key questions that are answered with diverse opinions representing all points on the political spectrum. Materials in each chapter include opinions in which authors clearly disagree as well as alternative opinions in which au- thors may agree on a broader issue but disagree on the pos- sible solutions. In this way, the content of each volume in *Current Controversies* mirrors the mosaic of opinions encoun- tered in society. Readers will quickly realize that there are many viable answers to these complex issues. By questioning each author's conclusions, students and casual readers can be- gin to develop the critical thinking skills so important to evaluating opinionated material.

Current Controversies is also ideal for controlled research. Each anthology in the series is composed of primary sources taken from a wide gamut of informational categories includ- ing periodicals, newspapers, books, U.S. and foreign govern- ment documents, and the publications of private and public organizations. Readers will find factual support for reports, debates, and research papers covering all areas of important issues. In addition, an annotated table of contents, an index, a book and periodical bibliography, and a list of organizations to contact are included in each book to expedite further re- search.

Perhaps more than ever before in history, people are con- fronted with diverse and contradictory information. During the Persian Gulf War, for example, the public was not only treated to minute-to-minute coverage of the war, it was also inundated with critiques of the coverage and countless analy- ses of the factors motivating U.S. involvement. Being able to sort through the plethora of opinions accompanying today's major issues, and to draw one's own conclusions, can be a complicated and frustrating struggle. It is the editors' hope that *Current Controversies* will help readers with this struggle.

Introduction

"Two issues that impact the different positions on drug policy are the perceived harms to the user of drugs and the perceived harms and benefits to society."

The issue of drug policy is one that countries around the world continue to debate. Broadly understood, according to *Merriam-Webster's Collegiate Dictionary*, a drug is "a substance other than food intended to affect the structure or function of the body." Under this definition, both legal pharmaceuticals such as penicillin and illegal street drugs such as cocaine qualify as drugs. Foods that affect the structure or function of the body, such as alcoholic beverages, coffee, tea, and some psychedelic mushrooms, may also be considered drugs. Some drugs are available as over-the-counter medicines, such as cough syrup. Other drugs are available only through a pharmacy with a doctor's prescription, such as penicillin and morphine. Drugs not considered medicine that are considered addictive, such as cocaine, are largely illegal throughout the world. Yet, other drugs that have addictive properties are widely legal with restrictions: Alcohol, in most countries, is legal but with age restrictions on use, as is nicotine, whether in the form of cigarettes, gum, or patches. In considering the issue of the legalization of drugs, the drugs most commonly under consideration are the widely illegal recreational drugs: marijuana, cocaine, heroin, and psychedelic drugs such as LSD.

Positions on the legalization of drugs such as marijuana, cocaine, heroin, and LSD are varied. Some call for the legalization of marijuana while continuing the prohibition of cocaine, heroin, and LSD. Others call for the legalization of all drugs. Among those who call for a change in the current U.S.

policy of prohibition on these drugs, not all favor complete legalization: Decriminalization is an option that lifts the current prohibition without complete legalization. Two issues that impact the different positions on drug policy are the perceived harms to the user of drugs and the perceived harms and benefits to society.

The harm of drug use to the user has always been one of the many drivers of drug policy. The concern is about both acute, or short-term, harm and chronic, or long-term, harm. For example, one concern about short-term heroin use is the risk of overdose from one use. Proponents of heroin prohibition often cite this potential harm as one reason for a complete restriction on heroin use. Yet, proponents of legalization may very well cite this same potential harm as a reason for regulated use in order to minimize the risk of overdose. Beyond the concern about acute effects such as overdose, there are concerns about the long-term effects of drug use, such as addiction. Proponents of cocaine prohibition may argue that cocaine has such strong addictive effects that a complete ban on its use is justified. Proponents of marijuana legalization, on the other hand, frequently compare the addictiveness of legal drugs, such as alcohol and nicotine, with marijuana to show that drug policy is inconsistent, given the relative harms of addiction.

Drug policy is also driven by the perceived harms and benefits to society. One of the nuanced distinctions in the drug legalization debate is between complete legalization and decriminalization. The argument for drug legalization is rarely absolute, as most currently legal drugs have a variety of restrictions affecting their production, sale, and use. These restrictions, such as the restriction on drinking alcohol and driving, are driven by the perceived benefits to society of such restrictions. Drug decriminalization calls for reduced control and penalties under the law for drug use, though not always for drug production. The idea behind drug decriminalization is to minimize the harms of drug use to society while stopping short of complete legalization. Proponents of this view argue that society suffers many harms from prohibition, such as increased violence and the costs of incarcerating drug users, which could be reduced by a policy of decriminalization. Yet, proponents of prohibition contend that criminalization is an important part of reducing drug use, drug production, and all associated harms to society.

The debate on drug policy will likely continue for years to come. Countries such as Argentina, the Czech Republic, and the Netherlands have adopted varying levels of decriminalization or legalization regarding certain drugs. In the United States, many states and localities have adopted relaxed policies toward marijuana use, and California is considering a voter initiative to legalize personal marijuana use. The current debates about drug legalization are explored in *Current Controversies: Drug Legalization,* shedding light on this fascinating and complicated contemporary issue.

CHAPTER 1

Is the Prohibition of Drugs Working?

Overview: The War on Drugs

Peter Katel

Peter Katel is a writer for CQ Researcher, *a periodical covering social and political issues. He received the Interamerican Press Association's Bartolomé Mitre Award for his coverage of drug trafficking.*

Pablo Rayo Montaño and Rita Faye Myers are about as different as two people could be. But America's 33-year-old war on drugs targeted them both with equal tenacity.

Montaño smuggled more than 15 tons of cocaine a month from Colombia to the United States and Europe, according to the U.S. Drug Enforcement Administration (DEA). His enterprise was so vast, the DEA says, he had his own "navy," including a small submarine.

Myers, by contrast, was anything but an international drug lord. A longtime drug addict, she is serving 21 years in an Alabama prison for forging a prescription for the synthetic opiate Dilaudid.

The War on Drugs

Since President Richard M. Nixon declared "war" on drugs in 1973, federal spending on the anti-drug campaign—stopping big-time drug smugglers and arresting users and sellers—has increased 30-fold—from $420 million in 1973 to $12.7 billion this fiscal year [2006].

And while drug use has shrunk since the peak years of the late 1970s and early '80s, half of the nation's 2005 high-school graduates reported having used an illegal drug at some point; the number of new heroin users has increased to more than 100,000 a year; and local officials across the country say meth-

Peter Katel, "War on Drugs: The Issues," *CQ Researcher*, vol. 16, no. 21, June 2, 2009, pp. 483–88. Copyright © 2009 by CQ Press, published by CQ Press, a division of Sage Publications, Inc. All rights reserved. Reproduced by permission.

amphetamine production and use are devastating their communities and over-burdening their resources.

But federal drug policy continues to focus on marijuana use because it is seen as a "gateway" to harder drugs, even as some drug experts call the gateway theory a myth. As a result of a shift in federal drug policy, drug arrests have nearly tripled since 1980. About 1.7 million people were arrested on drug charges in 2004, about 700,000 of them for marijuana. "The drug war met its goal of arrest and incarceration and seizures," says Kevin Zeese of Takoma Park, Md., president of Common Sense for Drug Policy and a longtime writer and activist on drug law, "yet the problem has gotten worse."

Drug-war advocates call such assertions absurd. The vast majority of Americans don't use illegal drugs, and "drug use by teens is going down," notes the Web site of the St. Petersburg, Fla.–based Drug Free America Foundation. "That's a failure?" As for marijuana, the country's most widely abused drug, the foundation cites 2004 testimony by National Institute on Drug Abuse (NIDA) Director Nora Volkow, who said "early exposure to marijuana increased the likelihood of a life filled with drug and addiction problems."

Such personal and social costs are reason enough to maintain the drug war, say enforcement advocates. "How are we doing in the war on cancer? Or crime? Or poverty?" asks Robert L. DuPont, former drug czar under presidents Gerald R. Ford and Jimmy Carter, when asked if the war on drugs is working. "Drugs are the only [societal] problem where [some critics say] the correct answer is supposed to be zero."

In fact, he says, drug prohibition has been far more effective in reducing drug use than the use of persuasion—without arrests—has been in reducing cigarette and alcohol use, which also impose serious personal and social costs.

However, critics of the government's approach to the drug war argue that officials should emphasize reducing demand by funding drug treatment programs rather than spending billions of dollars attacking the supply of drugs by trying to eradicate Latin American coca fields, halt illegal drug shipments and lock up users like Myers.

Demand Reduction

But the [George W.] Bush administration insists that it has struck the right balance and is reaping success on both fronts. "We put as much emphasis on driving down demand as on attacking supply," says David Murray, assistant to White House Office of National Drug Control Policy (ONDCP) Director John P. Walters. The administration vowed to reduce drug use among young people by 25 percent over five years, Murray explains. "We're four years out, and we're at a 19 percent reduction. In Colombia . . . cultivation [of drug crops] is down and their productivity is dropping."

But Sen. Charles E. Grassley, R-Iowa, chairman of the Senate International Narcotics Control Caucus, dismisses the ONDCP's drug-eradication statistics as "mumbo-jumbo."

Meanwhile, at home, drug-war strategy has evolved into a mixture of arrest, court-supervised drug treatment and—often in the case of repeat offenders like Myers—incarceration. Even some advocates of imprisonment concede that punishments for users can far outweigh the crimes, but they say the judicial system is frustrated by repeat offenders.

"This is a little, old woman who has a sixth-grade education—a pleasant, nice person who was an addict," says District Judge Orson L. "Pete" Johnson, after Myers appeared before him in February charged with smoking crack cocaine. That arrest violated her parole on the Dilaudid charge.

Circuit Judge Julian King of Talladega, Ala.—who had handed down Myers' 21-year sentence—acknowledges that Myers "has a sickness" but cites her record of past convictions, failed treatment, missed court dates and flouted probation rules. "I send people to drug rehab constantly," he explains, but "it's hard to treat someone unless the person is willing to seek help. She had been afforded help in the past, and it hadn't been very successful."

In drug-war jargon, Myers has not responded to "demand reduction"—drug prevention and treatment. Law-enforcement activities, especially those that target drug shipments and traffickers, are defined as "supply reduction." For 2007, President Bush is proposing boosting supply-side funding from about 62 percent in 2006 to about 65 percent of the anti-drug budget, while demand-reduction programs would drop from 38 percent to about 36 percent.

Supply Reduction

John Carnevale, an economist who served in the ONDCP during the [President Bill] Clinton administration, says that during Bush's six years in office, there has been "a real shift in resources" from demand reduction to supply reduction. Compared to 2001, when the last Clinton-era budget was in effect, he says, Bush's latest budget proposal would step up demand-side funding by about 2 percent, while supply-side funding will have jumped 64 percent. Meanwhile, Carnevale says, "I don't see much of an effect in terms of reducing consumption."

But Murray says looking at federal dollars alone is misleading, because federal agencies are better suited to supply-side work, while states and localities are better at treatment. "The federal government can't neglect the border," Murray says. "And the city of San Francisco doesn't send troops to Colombia to help eradicate coca."

Crop eradication aside, the DEA and other federal agencies are engaged in a constant battle with foreign and domestic traffickers. Along with Montaño's capture, results this year include the April arrests of 16 people in the United States and eight in Colombia in connection with an alleged money-laundering and drug-smuggling operation that funneled $7 million a week in drug profits back to South America. And the year began with discovery of a lighted, ventilated, 2,400-foot-long tunnel—along with two tons of marijuana—being used for smuggling drugs into the country under the border with Mexico.

Since the first drug court opened in Miami in 1989, more than 1,750 have been established nationwide handling at least 70,000 defendants a year.

Drug Courts

However, the Bush administration *is* proposing a major increase—from about $10 million to $69 million—in federal funds for "drug courts," which cropped up across the country in the 1990s. The courts were set up to keep drug offenders out of jail by providing a period of court-supervised treatment, during which defendants submit to periodic drug tests and often are required to get and keep a full-time job. Generally, their charges are dropped if they pass the drug tests, while defendants who fail the tests are jailed for short periods of time or face standard court proceedings where they might get longer jail terms.

Since the first drug court opened in Miami in 1989, more than 1,750 have been established nationwide handling at least 70,000 defendants a year. A 2005 Government Accountability Office (GAO) study found that recidivism by drug-court defendants can run 35 percent less than in conventional courts, although not all drug courts are that successful. The study noted that defendants run the gamut from nonviolent first-time arrestees to people with "extensive criminal histories" and records of failed drug treatment.

Even though drug courts generally have been successful at reducing recidivism, some analysts say they are part of the reason arrest rates have risen so steeply. More people are being arrested for minor drug charges, such as marijuana possession, today than in the past because the police know the non-jail drug court option exists, says Marc Mauer, assistant director of The Sentencing Project, a nonprofit that advocates eliminating sentencing disparities. "That's either good news or bad news, depending how you look at it."

Of the 500,000 inmates serving time on federal, state and local drug charges of all kinds, most weren't jailed just for possession. The Sentencing Project found that 54 percent of prisoners doing time on state drug charges were sentenced for trafficking, while 43 percent were charged with either possession or possession with intent to distribute.

The Prohibition on Marijuana

As for the most popular illegal drug, "Marijuana defendants are less likely to end up in prison," says Mauer. "[So] the system does filter out high cases and low cases to a certain extent." Still, some 30,000 state and federal prisoners are doing time for marijuana, he says, slightly fewer than half of whom are high-level players who'd been involved in smuggling, money-laundering or trafficking. More than 7,000 marijuana prisoners are nonviolent first offenders who weren't trafficking.

In any case, marijuana-prohibition advocates have already lost the war of ideas, contends Ethan Nadelmann, executive director of the New York–based Drug Policy Alliance. "We have a rising cultural acceptance of marijuana," he says, pointing out that 96 million Americans—about 40 percent of the population 12 years old and up—have tried pot at least once, according to government statistics.

Nevertheless, drug czar Walters made a point of announcing this year's drug-war strategy—with a continued focus on stopping marijuana use—in Denver, Colo., where citizens voted 54–46 percent last November to decriminalize possession of one ounce or less of marijuana. "Marijuana is the single biggest cause of [drug] treatment in this country by far," said Walters.

But Walters' continued emphasis on going after marijuana use is leading even some drug-war advocates to complain that the federal government is giving short shrift to the growing problem of methamphetamine abuse. "The ONDCP has done nothing but repeat its intention to provide a methamphetamine strategy," the House Government Reform Committee said in a March [2006] analysis of federal drug policy.

Harsh Sentences

Meanwhile, the popularity of hard-line strategies may be fading. In 2004, New York lawmakers reduced the state's notoriously harsh "Rockefeller" laws mandating lengthy sentences of even first-time offenders.

Still, law-enforcement officials acknowledge that street arrests, which account for the bulk of drug detentions, fall most heavily on poor neighborhoods, where many drug deals take place in the open. "What we do well is arrest and prosecute," says David Soares, elected as district attorney of New York's Albany County in 2004 as an opponent of the state's Rockefeller laws. "What we don't do well is stabilize these communities [which] are suffering from . . . a lot of poverty."

Those who advocate decriminalizing drugs argue that the urge to take mind-altering substances lies deep in the human psyche.

The Debate About Prohibition

As the drug war grinds on, it provokes some of these intensely debated questions:

Should drug use be treated as a law-enforcement issue or a public-health matter?

Those who advocate decriminalizing drugs argue that the urge to take mind-altering substances lies deep in the human psyche. Attempts to eradicate drug use are doomed and represent an impractical impulse to try to control natural behavior, say supporters of legalization.

"Law enforcement should be involved at the fringes— enforcing Driving Under the Influence, for instance," says Zeese of Common Sense for Drug Policy. "As far as personal consumption goes, the more important concern is making sure that people have access to health care if they get in trouble. But the vast majority don't end up needing treatment."

One veteran drug warrior doesn't mind conceding that point, even as he upholds the law-enforcement approach. "Not everybody who's smoked marijuana needs treatment," says DuPont, the former drug-policy director who runs two consulting companies on drugs in schools and the workplace. What they need, he says, is a solid reason to quit, and getting arrested is enough to scare many people straight.

They should quit, he says, because society shouldn't have to bear the enormous costs of drug abuse. A 2002 ONDCP report estimates that drug abuse costs the nation $180.9 billion a year in lost productivity and spending on law enforcement, prisons and health care.

Prohibition is what makes those costs so high, say decriminalization advocates.

Harm Reduction

"Our approach now is that we make it as dangerous as possible to use drugs," says Allan Clear, executive director of the New York–based Harm Reduction Coalition. "That's why so many people are living with HIV and Hepatitis C related to injection-drug use." Drug laws prohibit people from buying syringes over the counter, he said, so people have to share needles, adding to both infection rates.

The coalition provides training and advice to needle-exchange programs in New York and Oakland, Calif., which provide clean injecting tools to heroin, cocaine or methamphetamine addicts in return for used syringes. "Harm-reduction" doctrine accepts that some people will continue using drugs, notwithstanding the illegality. Hence, Clear says, "You must be able to help them protect themselves and their families from total destruction," while arresting those who commit crimes to finance their addictions.

Law-enforcement advocates—and some recovering addicts as well—argue that criminal penalties prevent drug trafficking from expanding and force drug abusers to get treatment—in effect, saving their lives. "After experiencing this environment for 60 or 90 days, they have these epiphanies," says a recovering addict at Regional Addiction Prevention Inc. (RAP), a 36-year-old treatment program based in Washington, D.C. "But someone [first] said, 'Your option is this, or I'm going to revoke your probation or parole.'"

Hubert Williams, president of the non-profit Police Foundation, favors police pressure but argues that it's not being aimed at the right target. "If we want to use the standard of the number of people we arrest—about 1.7 million people get busted every year—but these numbers deal with quantity not quality. We're busting people for use—not trafficking. We need a new strategy that doesn't focus on the ghetto and the inner city, . . . [one] that brings together intelligence and analyses on the big gangs—[like] the Bloods, the Crips, the Jamaican posses, Russian Mafia. Bust them and bring them down."

The Decriminalization Option

Nadelmann, of the Drug Policy Alliance, says drug use should be decriminalized, with police action reserved for those who harm other people. And even drug treatment shouldn't always be mandatory. "It's not even clear that drug use should be an issue of public health if it doesn't present public health problems," he says.

When drug use is defined as a crime, Nadelmann says, poor people inevitably bear the brunt of drug enforcement because better-off people with drug problems get sent to psychotherapists. Poor people get stuck with court-supervised programs in which success is measured by testing "clean" for drug use.

However, Albany County District Attorney Soares fears the effects of simply decriminalizing drugs. While he advocates sentencing reform and expanding treatment opportunities, he says, "I am not for legalization. I have seen the devastation alcohol has wreaked in communities. I don't believe in making more of these substances available."

RAP's staff trainer and clinical supervisor Rahman Abdullah—a recovered heroin addict—also opposes decriminalization. But he says policymakers don't seem to understand that the drug war has been accompanied by a steady climb in violence and desperation in poor communities, as each crop of street drug dealers is replaced by an even more violent generation. "All the young people born right now, they're going to start thinking that this is the norm, and they're going to take it a little further."

Supply and Demand

Should the federal government focus its drug-enforcement strategy on interdiction?

Tension has persisted for four decades between promoters of a "supply-side" approach to drug-control policy and those recommending a "demand-side" approach. Supply-siders say the government should focus on eradicating drug crops abroad and seizing drugs either being smuggled into the United States or domestically grown or manufactured. Demand-siders advocate reducing U.S. demand for illegal drugs by spending more money on addiction treatment and programs to persuade users to quit taking drugs and youngsters to refrain from taking them in the first place.

The federal government argues that cutting off the supply of drugs and shrinking the number of users are both essential. "These things have to be in balance," says Murray, drug czar Walters' assistant. "If [traffickers] don't have money, they can't buy protection. How do you attack the market? You can go after it one way or the other, but you'd better do both simultaneously; they augment each other."

Interdiction, or Cutting Supply

But some drug-war veterans say that supply-side spending has gotten far more attention from the Bush administration. As former Clinton ONDCP official Carnevale points out, interdiction funding increased dramatically—by $3.2 billion—between 2001 and Bush's proposed 2007 budget, while demand-reduction funding increased by only $49 million.

"You can see a real shift in resources. The shift is so dramatic, and in my mind irrational," says Carnevale, who, in fact, supports the war against drugs. "[But] I don't see much of an effort in terms of reducing consumption."

Moderate critics like Carnevale stop short of condemning supply-side efforts. "If we wanted to impact the amount of people using drugs," says Police Foundation president Williams, "then we've got to suppress the amount of drugs available for abuse."

Opponents of interdiction, on the other hand, are more blunt. "Interdiction and eradication have consistently made the drug problem worse," says Zeese, of Common Sense for Drug Policy. For example, he explains, after the [Ronald] Reagan administration shut down seaborne and airborne marijuana smuggling from Colombia in the early 1980s, "The Colombians switched to cocaine, which is more profitable and easier to smuggle. So we had a giant cocaine glut, which led to crack."

Because there was an excess of cocaine on the market, drug sellers aggressively began pushing crack cocaine—the cheaper, more addictive, smokable form of cocaine—which devastated America's inner cities in the late 1980s, triggering a crime wave characterized by drive-by shootings, teenagers killing each other in drug turf wars and unprecedented rates of drug addiction.

That record of violence raises the pressure on federal officials to stop the drug problem at the source of most illicit drugs—farmers' fields and clandestine laboratories in Latin America and Asia. But critics of the interdiction strategy say it can't possibly overcome socioeconomic imbalances between nations. "I don't blame any foreign country, especially a poor country, that exports drugs to a rich country that demands it," says Clear of the Harm Reduction Coalition.

And, though crop-eradication programs typically include programs to provide farmers with alternative crops, these are never as profitable, Clear says. "You have to offer farmers a viable alternative."

Tension has persisted for four decades between promoters of a "supply-side" approach to drug-control policy and those recommending a "demand-side" approach.

The Demand for Drugs

Even supply-reduction advocates like the Police Foundation's Williams concede that deeper issues are also at play. Demand-reduction proponents like Zeese insist that supply isn't the overriding issue. "At some point we have to begin to ask the question: What is it that makes Americans, particularly our youth, so much in need of escaping from the psychological environments in which they are situated?" he says.

But the moderates say advocates of both interdiction and demand reduction should acknowledge that drug use will always exist. Acting against supply "simply drives up the street price, and therefore increases the crime and all the other things that go along with it," says David Keene, chairman of the American Conservative Union (ACU), who quickly adds that doing nothing about supply also bothers him. "Given . . . human nature, you will never eradicate the problem; you want something that keeps it under control."

The moderates say advocates of both interdiction and demand reduction should acknowledge that drug use will always exist.

Like its predecessors, the Bush administration seems to share Keene's conclusion. The White House ONDCP's 2006 drug control strategy document speaks about "reducing" drug use, not eliminating it, and the agency says "healing drug users" is a priority.

Some fervent drug warriors voice skepticism. In a lengthy analysis of administration strategy, the House Committee on Government Reform, whose Criminal Justice, Drug Policy and Human Resources Subcommittee oversees drug-war efforts, concluded that the administration's rhetoric about balancing supply-side and demand-side programs was empty.

"Since prevention comprises only 11.7 percent of the entire FY [fiscal year] 2007 drug-control budget and represents a 19.3 percent decrease in prevention funding from that enacted in FY 2006, the committee questions the administration's claim that it has 'set a bold agenda' in its prevention efforts," the committee reported.

The U.S. Fight Against Illegal Drugs Is Working

Office of National Drug Control Policy

Established by the Anti-Drug Abuse Act of 1988, the White House Office of National Drug Control Policy (ONDCP) is a component of the executive office of the president that establishes policies, priorities, and objectives for the nation's drug control program.

In 2002, the President [George W. Bush] established ambitious goals for reversing a decade-long surge in illicit drug use in America: a 10 percent reduction in youth drug use in 2 years and a 25 percent reduction in youth drug use over 5 years. Since then, the President's *National Drug Control Strategy* has effectively guided the Nation's efforts to reduce illegal drug use, achieving an 11 percent reduction in youth drug use over the first 2 years and a 23 percent reduction in youth drug use over the first 5 years as measured by the *Monitoring the Future* (MTF) study.

A Decline in Drug Use

Seven years later, MTF's national survey of 8th, 10th, and 12th grade students indicates that current use of illicit drugs by youth has declined by 25 percent. However, it is the breadth and depth of these reductions in youth drug use that are particularly impressive. Marijuana use has fallen by 25 percent, and youth use of drugs such as MDMA/Ecstasy, LSD, and methamphetamine has dropped precipitously over the same period, cutting the current use of these dangerous drugs by more than 50 percent. Approximately 900,000 fewer young Americans are using illicit drugs today than when this Administration began.

National Drug Control Strategy: 2009 Annual Report, Office of National Drug Control Policy, 2009.

The importance of these dramatic changes in youth drug use patterns cannot be overemphasized. Studies indicate that young people who initiate drug use early in their teen years are at far greater risk of developing a drug dependency than those who initiate later in life. Moreover, young people who do not initiate drug use by age 18–20 are highly unlikely to develop a drug dependency problem in succeeding years, and this protective effect stays with them throughout their lives. By focusing on reducing drug use during this critical period in the lives of young people, we can positively impact the health and safety of Americans well into the future.

However, the substantial declines in drug use in America are not solely found among the youth of today and the adults of tomorrow. Current workforce drug testing data from Quest Diagnostics indicate that cocaine and methamphetamine use by adult Americans also may have turned a corner over the past several years. Positive drug tests for cocaine declined by 38 percent from June 2006 to June 2008, the latest date of available data. The percentage testing positive for methamphetamine—a form of amphetamines—had been rising quickly in the first half of the decade, but this percentage dropped by roughly 50 percent from 2005 to 2007. Overall, drug test positives indicate the lowest levels of drug use in the U.S. workforce since 1988.

Remaining Challenges

Although the dynamics of drug abuse in America have made a profound change for the better over the course of this Administration, challenges clearly remain. The *National Survey on Drug Use and Health* (NSDUH) indicates nearly 7 million Americans exhibit the diagnostic criteria for illicit drug abuse or dependence, with marijuana being by far the biggest contributor to the need for treatment.

According to NSDUH, more than one in four 12–17 year olds who report using marijuana in the past year display the characteristics of abuse or dependency. NSDUH also indicates that the risk of marijuana abuse or dependency for those aged 12 to 17 now exceeds that for alcohol and tobacco. Recent research suggests early marijuana use increases the risk of abuse or dependency on other drugs such as heroin and cocaine later in life. Research also confirms that marijuana use itself is a serious risk, not only due to its addictive potential but also due to recently identified connections between frequent marijuana use and mental illness.

The most recent NSDUH data show over two million people misused prescription drugs for the first time in the past year. This is more than the number of new marijuana users. Although not all new users will continue drug use in the future, the large number who are misusing prescription drugs for the first time is a cause for concern and action.

The *National Drug Control Strategy* has produced significant results over the course of this Administration. By building upon the tools that proved most effective in generating those results, we will sustain the progress we have made and rise to meet new challenges. This effort will continue to be guided by three national priorities: stopping initiation; reducing drug abuse and addiction; and disrupting the market for illegal drugs. . . .

Comprehensive and balanced drug policies can reduce the scale of both drug use and drug markets.

Stopping Initiation

The past eight years have shown that comprehensive and balanced drug policies can reduce the scale of both drug use and drug markets. Demand and supply reduction activities, including evidence-based prevention and early intervention programs, have resulted in fewer first time illicit drug users, significant reductions in youth drug use, and an increased perception of the health and social consequences associated with drug use.

Programs such as the Drug Free Communities Support Program, Random Student Drug Testing, the National Youth Anti-Drug Media Campaign, and Prescription Drug Monitoring Programs have contributed greatly to these outcomes and will continue to help drive down illegal drug use in America in 2009.

Every day, in towns and cities across the United States, parents, teachers, coaches, community leaders, law enforcement officials, and others are pushing back against illegal drug use. Among the most effective and sustainable measures are those that reduce the factors that can lead to drug use, including drinking, and strengthen the factors that can contribute to healthy communities. Now in its 11th year, the Drug Free Communities Support Program has helped hundreds of communities in their efforts to bring about sustainable changes in youth substance use at the local level.

The Drug Free Community Program

Drug Free Community (DFC) grants are designed to reduce substance use, including alcohol and tobacco, among youth, and to strengthen collaboration among various sectors in communities across America. Administered by the Office of National Drug Control Policy (ONDCP), and in partnership with the Department of Health and Human Services (HHS) Substance Abuse and Mental Health Services Administration (SAMHSA) through an interagency agreement, the program embodies the Administration's dedication to supporting the united efforts of young people, parents, educators, non-profits, law enforcement, employers, and other key constituents at the local level. The DFC program currently funds 769 grassroots community coalitions in all 50 States, the District of Columbia, Puerto Rico, Palau, American Samoa, and the U.S. Virgin Islands, with grants up to $125,000 per year for 5 years.

Since 1997, the program has awarded an estimated $450 million to prevent youth drug use. In 2009, DFC will initiate a five-year training plan for its grantees. In a public-private partnership between ONDCP, SAMHSA, and the National Coalition Institute at the Community Anti-Drug Coalitions of America, this plan is designed to ensure that all grantees have access to the valuable training they need, when they need it. This training will provide coalitions with important information on sustainability, cultural competence, and organizational management.

In September 2008, ONDCP released the findings of a national cross-site evaluation of the DFC program. After more than four years of research conducted by Battelle Memorial Institute's Centers for Public Health Research and Evaluation, it is now clear that DFC-funded coalitions are reducing youth drug use at a faster pace than non-funded communities across the country. DFC-funded communities also have lower instances of youth use of tobacco, alcohol, and marijuana, when compared to the national average. Evaluators are now able to point to research findings that show the DFC model as an effective tool in reducing youth drug use at the community level. ONDCP will continue its evaluation of the DFC program to try to determine the specific factors that contributed to the success of these grantee communities. . . .

Random student drug testing is one program among many that schools are using to prevent and address youth drug use.

Targeted Substance Use Prevention

When it comes to alcohol and drugs, young people are especially vulnerable, in part because of the significant health and social consequences of early drug use and drug-using behavior. Consequently, youth should be provided with an array of prevention activities—from an evidence-based substance abuse prevention curriculum to random drug testing—to shield them from drug-related harms.

Since the President endorsed random student drug testing in his 2004 State of the Union address, more than 130 schools or school districts have received funds through U.S. Department of Education grants to help develop or maintain random testing programs, and thousands more schools are implementing drug testing programs using other sources of funding. These schools have recognized the role of drug testing as a promising deterrent against some of the most dangerous drugs facing youth today.

To advance the implementation of effective research-based student drug testing programs as part of comprehensive school drug and alcohol abuse prevention initiatives, the Administration requested and received $1 million in Fiscal Year (FY) 2008 to support the establishment of a new Student Drug Testing Institute by the Department of Education. The Institute provides technical assistance to Student Drug Testing grantees, as well as information on best practices in program design and implementation to schools seeking to establish student drug testing programs in their communities. The Administration has requested an additional $1 million in FY 2009 to support the Institute's important efforts.

Random student drug testing is one program among many that schools are using to prevent and address youth drug use. ONDCP will work with relevant drug control agencies to assess whether the current array of evidence-based prevention programs needs adjustments to remain relevant and effective with new generations of students. . . .

National Youth Anti-Drug Media Campaign

The National Youth Anti-Drug Media Campaign is the government's largest public health communication effort. The

Campaign seeks to educate and enable the country's youth to reject illicit drug use, convince current youth users of drugs to stop using them, and to educate parents and other influential adults that their actions can make a difference in helping to decrease adolescent drug use.

Approximately 72 percent of the Campaign's funding is allocated to purchase advertising time and space in youth, adult, and ethnic media outlets, including national and cable TV, radio, newspapers, magazines, out-of-home media (such as movies), and the Internet. The Partnership for a Drug-Free America recruits advertising agencies from around the country to provide pro-bono creative services to develop new ad campaigns. All television advertisements are subject to a rigorous process of qualitative and quantitative testing, ensuring— before they are ever seen—that the advertisements are credible and have the intended effect on awareness, attitudes, and behaviors.

The teen brand, Above the Influence, specifically draws the connection between substance use and the negative influences that surround it, both the influence of the drug itself and the social influences that can encourage its use.

Working closely with source countries is at the core of our strategy to disrupt the illegal drug supply chain.

While paid and matched advertising allows the Campaign to reach audiences with anti-drug messages on a national level, public communications outreach is critical to augmenting and amplifying the messages in ways that resonate with various audiences. This communications support includes maintaining Web sites, convening roundtable discussions with experts in the field, holding briefings with media, and developing partnership opportunities with nationally recognized organizations and companies to extend the reach of the Campaign's messages.

In 2009, the Campaign will continue to address prescription drug abuse through a national campaign to teach parents about the risky abuse of prescription drugs by young people. It will also continue its effort to reduce demand for methamphetamine by promoting prevention and treatment within the most at-risk regions of the country. . . .

Disrupting the Market for Illegal Drugs

The global drug trade exacts a terrible toll on the American people, threatening their families, their finances, and their freedoms. The illicit drug trade also poses a serious threat to our national security due to its ability to destabilize and corrupt governments and to diminish public safety in regions vital to U.S. interests. The ill-gotten profits and nefarious alliances cultivated by the drug trade also facilitate the activities of terrorists and organized criminals worldwide.

The United States confronts these threats through a combination of law enforcement investigation, interdiction, diplomatic efforts, targeted economic sanctions, financial programs and investigations, and institutional development initiatives focused on disrupting all segments of the illicit drug market, from the fields and clandestine laboratories where drugs are produced, to the streets of our communities where they directly threaten our citizens. Domestically, State, local, and tribal law enforcement cooperation are supported by Federal initiatives such as the High Intensity Drug Trafficking Area (HIDTA) and the Organized Crime Drug Enforcement Task Force (OCDETF) programs. These efforts are supplemented by the work of the DEA [Drug Enforcement Administration] Mobile Enforcement Team and U.S. Immigration and Customs Enforcement's (ICE) Border Enforcement Security Task Force (BEST) programs, as well as by the work of Federal agents operating out of DEA and ICE field offices across the Nation. Improved interagency coordination and technological enhancements are strengthening our defenses along our national borders. Internationally, the critical partnerships among the law enforcement, interdiction, and international development agencies of the United States and of our allies are increasing the risks and reducing the rewards for drug traffickers and narco-terrorists around the globe. Working closely with source countries is at the core of our strategy to disrupt the illegal drug supply chain, as it is in the source zone that we can remove the greatest amounts of drugs and profits from the system.

The domestic and international partnerships forged during this Administration are creating more agile and effective responses to disrupt the illicit drug markets that threaten the health, safety, and security of the citizens of the United States. The National Drug Intelligence Center's 2009 *National Drug Threat Assessment* describes historic disruptions in the cocaine and methamphetamine markets as a result of cumulative progress in Colombia, the transit zone, Mexico, and on the Southwest Border. Challenges remain, and surely new ones will emerge, but the past seven years have yielded meaningful achievements and important lessons learned. . . .

The Need for a Global Approach

While we have made significant progress over the last eight years in reducing the demand for and availability of illegal drugs in the United States, challenges remain both at home and abroad. For many years there has been a consensus, both in our own Nation and internationally, that illicit drug abuse has significant social and health consequences [and so] requires strict regulation. That consensus, although still strong, has come under attack internationally. Although decades of research suggest that balanced drug policies are working, well-funded legalization advocates continue to promote their views aggressively at international forums. To ensure that strong, effective international drug policies are maintained, it is essential that experts in the effectiveness of drug prevention, education, and treatment efforts step forward to educate the international community. Fortunately, a renewed international movement against drugs is emerging.

Our nation is moving steadily in the right direction, both domestically and internationally, in the fight against illegal drugs.

In September 2008, 600 representatives of anti-drug nongovernmental organizations gathered in Stockholm, Sweden for the first World Forum Against Drugs (WFAD) conference. After the successful completion of the conference and the signing of a declaration, WFAD organizers announced their intention to create a permanent organization to combat drug legalization efforts around the world through annual meetings, publications, and participation in international meetings such as the United Nations CND [Commission on Narcotic Drugs]. This group shows promise as a constructive partner in the effort to reduce drug use, production, and trafficking around the world.

This new commitment in the international community could not have come at a better time. This year marks the completion of the review by Member States and international organizations of the progress made towards the accomplishment of ambitious anti-drug goals set ten years ago at a United Nations General Assembly Special Session. In March 2009 high level government officials from around the world will gather in Vienna to review the world's progress. The United States and like-minded partners from every region of the world have been working to develop plans to move forward by building on the initial 1998 goals. The March meeting is expected to result in a renewed commitment by all to combat drug use, trafficking, and production.

The evidence produced by the array of data systems we use to measure progress makes it clear that our Nation is moving steadily in the right direction, both domestically and internationally, in the fight against illegal drugs. The past eight years of counterdrug efforts demonstrate that when we as a Nation work together to solve problems, those problems can be successfully confronted and made smaller. This progress is the cumulative result not just of the heroic efforts of law enforcement officers, parents, teachers, coaches, and other community leaders, but of the decisions of hundreds of thousands of individuals not to use drugs. This progress is real, but it cannot be sustained without the continued hard work of communities throughout America and our partners around the world.

The International Ban on Illicit Drugs Should Continue

United Nations Office on Drugs and Crime

The United Nations Office on Drugs and Crime fights against illicit drugs and international crime on a global level, funded by contributions from United Nations member states.

Last year's [2008] *World Drug Report* reviewed 100 years of drug control efforts, documenting the development of one of the first international cooperative ventures designed to deal with a global challenge. This pioneering work brought together nations with very different political and cultural perspectives to agree on a topic of considerable sensitivity: the issue of substance abuse and addiction. Despite wars, economic crises, and other cataclysmic events of state, the global drug control movement has chugged steadily forward, culminating in a framework of agreements and joint interventions with few precedents or peers in international law.

International Drug Control

Today, a number of substances are prohibited in the domestic legislation of almost every country. As discussed below, this unanimity has created a bulwark shielding millions from the effects of drug abuse and addiction. In the past, many of these substances were legally produced and, in some cases, aggressively marketed, to devastating effect. The collective nations of the world have agreed that this state of affairs was unacceptable, and have created an international control system that allows crops such as opium poppy to be produced for medical use, with very little diversion to the illicit market.

Despite this achievement, drug control efforts have rarely proceeded according to plan. There have been reversals and

United Nations Office on Drugs and Crime, "2: Confronting Unintended Consequences," *World Drug Report*. New York: United Nations, 2009, pp. 163–166.

set-backs, surprising developments and unintended consequences. Traffickers have proven to be resilient and innovative opponents and cultivators difficult to deter. The number, nature, and sources of controlled substances have changed dramatically over the years. None of this could have been predicted at the outset.

But then, very little has been simple or smooth about developments in international affairs over the last century. Other international problems—including poverty, war, weapons proliferation and infectious disease—have defied early projections of a swift resolution. Some efforts have been more successful than others, but, in all cases, the learning process could be described as "challenging". Today, the enterprise of global coordination and cooperation remains a work in progress. Tremendous gains have been made, however, and the need for collaborative solutions to the problems facing us all is greater than ever before.

Oddly, of all areas of international cooperation, drug control is uniquely subject to calls that the struggle should be abandoned.

International Consensus on Drug Control

Oddly, of all areas of international cooperation, drug control is uniquely subject to calls that the struggle should be abandoned. Despite equally mixed results in international interventions, no one advocates accepting poverty or war as inevitable. Not so with drugs, where a range of unintended consequences have led some to conclude that the only solution is to legalise and tax substances like cannabis, cocaine, ecstasy, methamphetamine, and heroin.

The strongest case against the current system of drug control is not the financial costs of the system, or even its effectiveness in reducing the availability of drugs. The strongest case against drug control is the violence and corruption associated with the black market. The main problem is not that drug control efforts have failed to eliminate drug use, an aspirational goal akin to the elimination of war and poverty. It is that in attempting to do so, they have indirectly enriched dangerous criminals, who kill and bribe their way from the countries where drugs are produced to the countries where drugs are consumed.

Of course, the member states of the United Nations created the drug conventions, and they can modify or annul them at will. But the Conventions would have to be undone the way they were done: by global consensus. And to date, there are very few international issues on which there has been so much positive consensus as drug control. Drug control was the subject of broad-based international agreements in 1912, 1925, 1931, 1936, 1946, 1948, and 1953, before the creation of the standing United Nations Conventions in 1961, 1971, and 1988. Nearly every nation in the world has signed on to these Conventions.

If currently illegal substances were made legal, their popularity would surely increase, perhaps reaching the levels of licit addictive substances, increasing the related morbidity and mortality.

The Argument for Legalization

Nonetheless, there remains a serious and concerned group of academics and civil society organisations who feel the present system causes more harm than good. Plans for drug "legalisation" are diverse, and often fuzzy on the details, but one of the most popular alternative models involves taxation and control in a manner similar to tobacco and alcohol. This approach has appeal of ideological consistency, since all these addictive substances are treated in the same way.

The practice of banning certain addictive substances while permitting and taxing others is indeed difficult to defend based on the relative harmfulness of the substances themselves. Legal addictive substances kill far more people every year than illegal ones—an estimated 500 million people alive today will die due to tobacco. But this greater death toll is not a result of the licit substances being pharmacologically more hazardous than the illicit ones. This greater death toll is a direct result of their being legal, and consequently more available. Use rates of illicit drugs are a fraction as high as for legal addictive drugs, including among those who access the legal drugs illegally (i.e. young people). If currently illegal substances were made legal, their popularity would surely increase, perhaps reaching the levels of licit addictive substances, increasing the related morbidity and mortality.

Is the choice simply one of drug-related deaths or drug-market-related deaths? Some palliative measures would be available under a system of legalisation that are not available today. If drugs were taxed, these revenues could be used to fund public health programmes aimed at reducing the impact of the increase in use. Addicts might also be more accessible if their behaviour were decriminalised. With bans on advertising and increasingly restrictive regulation, it is possible that drug use could be incrementally reduced, as tobacco use is currently declining in most of the developed world.

Protecting Developing Countries

Unfortunately, most of this thinking has indeed been restricted to the developed world, where both treatment and capacity to collect taxes are relatively plentiful. It ignores the role that global drug control plays in protecting developing countries from addictive drugs. Without consistent global policy banning these substances, developing countries would likely be afflicted by street drugs the way they are currently afflicted by growing tobacco and alcohol problems.

In most developing countries, street drugs are too scarce and expensive for most consumers. They are scarce and expensive because they are illegal. Today, traffickers concentrate on getting almost all of the cocaine and heroin produced to high-value destinations, placing the burden of addiction on those well suited to shoulder it, at least financially. If these pressures were removed, lower value markets would also be cultivated with market-specific pricing, as they presently are for most consumer goods.

For example, cocaine use in the countries where cocaine is actually produced is less than half as high as in many European countries or the United States. This could easily change. Bolivia is a poor country where 42% of the population lives on less than US$2 per day and which produces about 10% of the global cocaine supply. According to reported figures, cocaine in Bolivia was US$9 per gram in 2005, about 10% of the price in the United States. But GDP [gross domestic product] per capita was 42 times higher in the US than in Bolivia, so the price was effectively four times higher in Bolivia.

In contrast, 27% of the adult population of Bolivia smokes cigarettes daily. A pack of cigarettes was priced at just US$0.62 at official exchange rates in 2006, so even the poor find an imported addictive substance more affordable than the locally-produced one. Bolivia is not unique in this respect: in many poor countries, more than 10% of household expenditure is for tobacco.

There is no reason why both drug control and crime prevention cannot be accomplished with existing resources.

An Analogy with Tobacco

Indeed, the spread of tobacco to the developing world gives a hint of what could happen if other addictive substances were made legal. Many transition countries have much higher tobacco use prevalence than the richer ones, and Africa's tobacco market is presently growing by 3.5% per year, the fastest rate in the world. By 2030, more than 80% of the world's tobacco deaths will occur in developing countries. These countries can ill-afford this burden of disease. They are even less capable of giving up a share of their productive work force to more immediately debilitating forms of addiction.

"Vice taxes" are also used to control the spread of legal addictive drugs, making them more expensive and thus reducing demand. But again, capacity to enforce these taxes is less in developing countries, and high taxes generate large shadow markets, as illustrated by tobacco markets today. Recent estimates suggest 10% or more of global tobacco consumption is untaxed, and that the illicit share of the market is particularly pronounced in Africa (15%) and Latin America (20%). An estimated 600 billion cigarettes are smuggled each year. If these were priced at just a dollar a pack, this would represent a global market worth US$30 billion, comparable to the US$65 billion market for illicit opiates and US$71 billion market for cocaine. As with illicit drugs, illicit tobacco has been used to fund violence in places as diverse as the Balkans and West Africa.

The universal ban on illicit drugs thus provides a great deal of protection to developing countries, and must be maintained. At the same time, the violence and corruption associated with drug markets is very real, and must be addressed. Fortunately, there is no reason why both drug control and crime prevention cannot be accomplished with existing resources, if the matter is approached in a strategic and coordinated manner.

Drug Control and Crime Prevention

Drug addiction represents a large social cost, a cost we seek to contain through the system of international drug control. But this system itself has its costs, and these are not limited to the expenditure of public funds. International drug control has produced several unintended consequences, the most formidable of which is the creation of a lucrative black market for controlled substances, and the violence and corruption it generates.

Drug control generates scarcity, boosting prices out of proportion to production costs. Combined with the barriers of illegality and prevention efforts, scarcity and high prices have helped contain the spread of illicit drugs. This has kept drugs out of the hands of an untold number of potential addicts. At the same time, however, high prices allow transnational traffickers to generate obscene profits, simply for being willing to shoulder the risk of defying the law.

Given the money involved, competition for the opportunity to sell is often fierce, resulting in small wars on the streets of marginalised areas in the developed and the developing world alike. Profits are ploughed back into increasing the capacity for violence and into corrupting public officials. Together, violence and corruption can drive away investment and undermine governance to the point that the rule of law itself becomes questionable.

As a result, some have argued that the costs of controlling illicit drugs outweigh the benefits—in effect, that the side effects are so severe that the treatment is worse than the disease. But this is a false dilemma. It is incumbent on the international community to achieve both objectives: to control illicit drugs and to limit the costs associated with this control. More creative thinking is needed on ways of reducing the violence and corruption associated with containing the drug trade. Progress must be made toward simultaneously achieving the twin goals of drug control and crime prevention.

Restrictive Drug Policies Are Working and Must Continue

Robert L. DuPont

Robert L. DuPont is the president of the Institute for Behavior and Health, Inc., a former director of the National Institute on Drug Abuse, and White House drug chief from 1973 to 1978.

The *Economist* in its March 7–13, 2009 cover story, "How to Stop the Drug Wars," has escalated 20 years of increasing support for legalizing illegal drugs by calling this the "least bad solution." Its position on this topic has evolved to the point that it now disputes two popular pro-legalization myths:

1. *The Economist* acknowledges that harm reduction—steps like giving clean needles to intravenous drug users, decriminalization of marijuana and medical marijuana— does not reduce drug trafficking because it does not reduce financial incentives for the illegal drug market. In fact, because these steps make it easier, cheaper and safer to use illegal drugs, they build illegal drug markets.

2. *The Economist* states that outright drug legalization would increase the use of currently illegal drugs.

Though greatly understated, these are important admissions.

Prohibition Has Not Failed

"Prohibition has failed," opens the lead article, one of a collection of reports in this issue. The facts are otherwise. On the contrary, restrictive drug policies are working reasonably well. In the US, illegal drug use has been cut from 14% of Americans aged 12 and older in 1979 to 8% in 2007. Far from a fail-

Robert L. DuPont, "What's Wrong with Legalizing Illegal Drugs?" Institute for Behavior and Health, Inc., March 24, 2009. Reproduced by permission.

ure this is a result that any public health program can envy. The *Economist*'s broadside coincides with the 100th anniversary of the 1909 Shanghai treaty, the first international effort to curb opium traffic. The Shanghai treaty saved China, the Philippines and other Asian countries from what had become a devastating opium epidemic, a fact *The Economist* leaves unstated.

Restrictive drug policies are working reasonably well.

The analogy to legal gambling is instructive. Today no one talks about curbing illegal gambling as a goal of legal gambling because the data is clear: legal gambling builds the business of illegal gambling. The same would be true for the legal availability of formerly illegal drugs. By making drugs legal there would be a large increase in illegal drug use (as there has been in illegal gambling). The illegal drug suppliers would thrive by selling more potent products outside of the taxation and restrictions that all governments would place on a regulated and legal drug supply.

No Realistic Proposal for Legalization

In the past, proposals to legalize drugs have suffered from the same pitfall into which the current series of articles in *The Economist* finds itself. Virtually the entire content is devoted to the costs of keeping drugs illegal. For example *The Economist*'s headline story, "Prohibition has failed" is followed by page after page of horror stories about drug trafficking. All of the legalization proposals neglect to deliver a comprehensive plan for what to legalize (all drugs? all doses? all routes of administration?). The legalization devil is in the never-described details. The reason a fleshed-out proposal to legalize all drugs is not to be found in this or any other publication is that it cannot be done. Any realistic proposal for legalization would be so frightening and so obviously destructive that it would be a political non-starter, or so limited that it would be irrelevant to the goal of eliminating illegal drug trafficking.

To fairly evaluate the current restrictive international drug laws we need a realistic assessment of the risks of making drugs of abuse more easily available. As a group these drugs pose far greater risks than alcohol or tobacco because they are so much more powerfully reinforcing. If the US were to legalize the drugs that are now illegal, the number of users would increase for each drug to numbers similar to alcohol and tobacco. Today in the US there are 127 million current users of alcohol but only 20 million current users of all illegal drugs combined. That contrast is the result of the effect of restrictive drug policies, not the relative attractiveness of the drugs. Think for a minute about what this country might be like with 50 million marijuana smokers, 50 million methamphetamine users, and/or 50 million cocaine users. The list of candidate drugs is as long as the potential costs are horrific. Then think of this fact: today the total social costs of alcohol and tobacco are each greater than the social costs of all the currently illegal drugs combined. Does the way we treat these legal drugs offer an attractive model for any, let alone all, illegal drugs?

New drug policies must be smarter and more effective in reducing illegal drug use.

The canary in the coal mine for drug legalization is found in the current explosive growth of the abuse of prescribed opiates. In the US, deaths from prescription opiates now exceed the deaths from heroin and cocaine combined. Additionally, every year since 2005 more Americans have started using these drugs without having their own valid prescription than have begun using marijuana. Within the rapidly growing prescription drug problem there is little or no illegal trafficking and yet the health consequences are tragic. This experience shows that it is the use of drugs that creates most of the costs of the drug problem and not as *The Economist* and other critics of restrictive drug policies would have us believe, that the costs are a consequence of drug "prohibition," including illegal drug trafficking,

The Need for New Policies

The great danger in today's drug policy debate is not that the world will legalize all of the currently illegal drugs as *The Economist* encourages. It is that the determined and well-financed efforts to remove restrictive drug policies will sideline the important policy role of the criminal justice system, and that governments will provide drugs as well as drug-using paraphernalia to drug users. Such "harm reduction" policies, which to its credit *The Economist* dismisses, are the real drug policy threat because they substantially worsen the drug problems of the world by increasing illegal drug use.

New drug policies must be smarter and more effective in reducing illegal drug use. Curbing the demand for illegal drugs must be their central goal. New and better policies can greatly improve current performance of drug abuse prevention which, far from failing, has protected millions of people from the devastating effects of wider use of the drugs that are illegal today.

The Institute for Behavior and Health, Inc. is dedicated to identifying, promoting and evaluating new ideas to reduce illegal drug use. Legalization of currently illegal drugs is not on our list of promising new ideas because legalization of these drugs is neither new nor promising.

3 Main Points

The War on Drugs Was lost before it began

1) Fueled by hate & propaganda

2) Waste of Money

3) Holds back Progress

Holds back together
when moved is swiveled
position will becomes
colateral damage

The War on Drugs
Is Not Working

Radley Balko

Radley Balko is a senior editor at Reason *magazine and* Reason
.com.

At around 6pm on January 27 of last year [2008], 80-year-
old Isaac Singletary spotted a couple of drug dealers attempting to do business on his front lawn. It wasn't the first
time. Singletary, described by relatives as territorial and a bit
crotchety, did what he'd done in the past. He grabbed his gun,
and walked out on to his lawn to scare them off. Problem is,
this time the men weren't drug dealers. They were undercover
Jacksonville, Florida police posing as drug dealers. They had
come on to Singletary's property to bait possible drug offenders. When he brandished his gun, the police shot Singletary
four times, once in the back. He died a short time later. A
subsequent investigation by Florida's attorney general cleared
the officers who shot Singletary of any wrongdoing.

Collateral Damage

Singletary wasn't a drug dealer. Jacksonville Sheriff John Ruth-
erford described him as "an honest citizen trying to do good."
Florida Governor Charlie Crist visited Jacksonville a few days
later. When asked by a reporter about Singletary's death, Crist
euphemistically called it one of the "challenges in fighting
crime."

Singletary is far from the first innocent person to die for
the war on drugs, and he's nowhere near the last. But let's call
Singletary's death what it is: collateral damage. Like the collateral damage of military wars overseas—innocents inadvert-

ently killed by bombs, bullets, and missiles aimed at legitimate targets—Singletary's a victim only because he happened to live in close proximity to the government's intended target, in this case, drug offenders. And like the civilian casualties of military wars, Singletary's death won't do a thing to cause the people who run this war to rethink their priorities. Because for them, the ultimate goal is more important than the innocent lives they may take along the way. As Governor Crist said, Singletary's death is really little more than a "challenge" on the journey to a drug-free Florida.

The drug war's aim is to stop people from getting high.

But whatever you may think of the legitimacy of some of America's military wars, past or present, they're waged under at least the pretense that they're necessary to defeat a foreign aggressor that poses a real threat to U.S. security. The drug war's aim is to stop people from getting high.

The War on Drugs

When [former U.S. president] Richard Nixon first uttered the phrase "war on drugs" in 1971, he chose his words carefully. Government declarations of war signal to the country that the threat we're facing is so perilous, so grave, so existential, that in order to defeat it, we should prepare to give up some basic freedoms, to make significant sacrifices, and—yes—to accept the inevitable collateral damage we may endure on our way to victory. It so happens that to Nixon, that threat was dirty hippies smoking marijuana and urban blacks strung out on heroin.

It was during the [Ronald] Reagan administration that the "war on drugs" got a lot more literal. [First Lady] Nancy Reagan's "Just Say No" campaign was backed by an administration of culture warriors ready to settle remnant grudges from the 1960s, an aggressive justice department, and an eager and compliant Congress. Every 1980s celebrity overdose or high-profile drug abuse story sent both parties scrambling to see who could pass the most odious and draconian new drug bill. The climax came in 1986, when [University of] Maryland basketball phenom and Boston Celtics draft pick Len Bias died of a cocaine overdose. Eric Sterling, who helped write much of that legislation and is now an activist for reforming the drug laws, likened the frenzy to a stampeding herd of wildebeests. From journalist Dan Baum's terrific history of the drug war, *Smoke and Mirrors*:

> Sterling had once seen a film shooting Tanzania; a million wildebeest grazing peacefully, until one of them started running. Assuming danger, a few more joined in, and in no time, the whole heard was stampeding wildly, trampling the sick and the slow, laying waste to the flora and fauna alike in a senseless headlong panic. Those images kept occurring to him as he watched Congress in the weeks following Len Bias's death.

The wildebeests have been charging in a blind gallop ever since. Through the Reagan, [Bill] Clinton, and both [the George H.W. and George W.] Bush administrations, both major political parties have exacerbated and expanded what is arguably the most destructive and wasteful government policy of the last 40 years. . . .

The drug war touches nearly every area of American life—certainly all facets of U.S. public policy. But here are a few areas where drug prohibition has done the most damage:

There are around 50,000 SWAT deployments per year today in America, and they're primarily used to serve drug warrants.

Police Militarization

In the 1980s, the "war" part of the drug war got very real. America's long (and wise) constraint on using the military for domestic policing began to blur, as states deployed National Guard troops to search for marijuana hidden in fields and forests and, in some cases, to patrol drug-riddled inner cities. The line between cop and soldier further blurred when President Reagan authorized active-duty elite military units to train with narcotics police, and then again with the exploding use of paramilitary SWAT [special weapons and tactics] teams in America.

Only a handful of police departments had SWAT teams in the 1970s, and they were only deployed in total a few hundred times per year. That number soared to around 4,000 per year by the early 1980s. There are around 50,000 SWAT deployments per year today in America, and they're primarily used to serve drug warrants.

By the late 1980s, Congress had opened up the Pentagon's cache of surplus military equipment for civilian police departments across the country to scavenge, again driven largely by the drug war. Millions of pieces of equipment designed for use on the battlefield—including guns, tanks, armored personnel vehicles, helicopters, grenade launchers, and armor—would now be used on American streets, against American citizens. Parallel to the rise of SWAT teams was the rise of the "no-knock raid" which sent cops barreling into private homes to look for dope, a particularly aggressive and violent method of policing that has since left behind a predictable trail of tragedy.

As many police officers internalize the mentality that they're fighting a "war," police-community relations have soured, and many officers have adopted the "us or them" mindset typically seen in soldiers. Here's former Kansas City and San Jose police chief Joseph McNamara, in a 2006 op-ed for the *Wall Street Journal*:

> Simply put, the police culture in our country has changed.
> An emphasis on "officer safety" and paramilitary training
> pervades today's policing, in contrast to the older culture,

which held that cops didn't shoot until they were about to be shot or stabbed. Police in large cities formerly carried revolvers holding six .38-caliber rounds. Nowadays, police carry semi-automatic pistols with 16 high-caliber rounds, shotguns and military assault rifles, weapons once relegated to SWAT teams facing extraordinary circumstances. Concern about such firepower in densely populated areas hitting innocent citizens has given way to an attitude that the police are fighting a war against drugs and crime and must be heavily armed.

The military's task is to conquer and annihilate a foreign enemy. The police are charged with protecting the public order, but without sacrificing the rights of the citizenry. It's dangerous to conflate the two. But that seems to be where we're headed. Our politicians have dressed our police like soldiers, trained them in paramilitary tactics, given them military weapons and armor, and told them they're fighting a "war." We shouldn't be surprised if and when some police officers take that message to heart. . . .

The Rule of Law

"The Fourth Amendment has been virtually repealed by court decisions," Yale law professor Steven Duke told *Wired* magazine in 2000, "most of which involve drug searches."

The rise of the aforementioned no-knock raid is one example, as is the almost comically comprehensive list of reasons for which you can be legally detained and invasively searched for drugs at an airport. In many areas of the country, police are conducting "administrative searches" at bars and clubs, in which an obvious search for criminality is cloaked in the guise of a regulatory inspection, obviating the need for a search warrant.

But the drug war has undermined the rule of law in other ways than its evisceration of the Fourth Amendment. Take the bizarre concept of asset forfeiture, an attack on both due process and property rights. Under the asset forfeiture laws passed by Congress in the 1980s (then reformed in 2000), *property can be found guilty of a drug crime*. The mere presence of an illicit substance in your home or car can allow the government to seize your property, sell it, and keep the proceeds. The onus is then on you to prove you obtained your property legally. Even the presence of an illicit drug isn't always necessary. The government has seized and kept cash from citizens under the absurd argument that merely carrying large amounts of cash is enough to trigger suspicion. If you can't prove where you got the money, you lose it.

The drug war has undermined the rule of law in less obvious ways, too. As was the case with alcohol prohibition, and is the case with the prohibition of any consensual crime, the people we ask to police these crimes often have to break the very laws they're enforcing. The presence of large sums of unaccounted money can be tempting, as we've seen in the countless stories of drug cops gone bad.

In many urban areas, the drug war has completely eradicated respect for the rule of law.

But the drug war breeds corruption in more mundane ways, too. Politicians and prosecutors want statistics—lots of arrests, big busts, and lots of drug seizures. The temptation for even well-meaning cops to take shortcuts looms large. We saw this in Atlanta in 2006 when a botched drug raid led to the death of 92-year-old Kathryn Johnston. Subsequent investigations revealed that not only did police in that case lie about nearly every aspect of Johnston's case, but that lying on search warrants to make the quick bust was common among Atlanta's narcotics cops.

The Informant System

The cops in the Johnston case also lied about their use of a confidential informant, another common temptation in drug policing. Police abuse of the drug informant system led to the high-profile scandals in Tulia and Hearne, Texas as well as other scandals in St. Louis, Cleveland, and elsewhere.

The use of street informants is bad enough. But there's also the problem of jailhouse informants, convicts facing long sentences who testify against drug suspects in exchange for a reduction in their time behind bars. Despite the obvious shortcomings in their trustworthiness—they're cons who have everything to gain by lying, and nothing to lose—countless innocents have been wrongly convicted on the word of jailhouse snitches.

These inherent problems with the informant system have given rise to the "Stop Snitch'n" movement, which, whatever you may think of it, has revealed the troubling extent to which entire communities in America have completely given up on the people charged with protecting them, even when it comes to helping with investigations of violent crime. Many understandably find the "Stop Snitch'n" movement repugnant, but there's no question that it's symptomatic of a larger problem: In many urban areas, the drug war has completely eradicated respect for the rule of law.

Crime, Violence, and Prison

If you look at a graph of the U.S. murder rate going back to about 1915, you'll notice a few interesting patterns: There's a spike at around 1919, just at the onset of alcohol prohibition. The graph then takes a dramatic dip in 1933, just after the repeal of prohibition. There's then another spike in the late 1960s, just as Richard Nixon took office and fired the first shots of his war on drugs. That spike falls in the 1970s as President [Jimmy] Carter took a less militant approach to drug prohibition, but then with Reagan's reinvigorated war in the 1980s, it begins another upward ascent.

This shouldn't be surprising. Prohibitions create black markets, and black markets spawn crime. Drug prohibition, then, spawns violent crime. There's a reason we don't often hear about a Michelob [beer] deal gone bad. Because alcohol is legal, there are no turf wars, no sour deals, no smuggling operations to defend.

One in 100 Americans today is behind bars. That number by far and away leads the world, and is at its highest point in American history. About 350,000 of the approximately 3 million Americans behind bars are there for nonviolent drug crimes (trafficking or possession). It would be impossible to approximate, but countless others are undoubtedly in for violent or property crimes that are by-products of drug prohibition. The drug war has turned entire neighborhoods into, well, war zones. If the temptation of the drug trade can be too much for some police officers, you can imagine the allure for a young urban kid wasting away in an awful public school with few other prospects.

It's difficult to know what effect the exploding prison population will have on American society going forward, but it certainly can't be good.

Hundreds of thousands of people who've victimized no one will spend a good deal of their lives in prison alongside hardened criminals, then face lives on the outside limited by their status as convicted felons. . . .

Even if the drug war were working . . . you'd have a difficult time arguing that the benefits would be worth the costs.

A Failed War

Even if the drug war were working—even if all the horrible things the federal government says are caused by illicit drugs were accurate (and some of them admittedly are), and even if the war on drugs were proving successful in eradicating or

even significantly diminishing our access to those drugs—
you'd have a difficult time arguing that the benefits would be
worth the costs.

But the kicker is, of course, that it isn't working. Most of
the federal government claims about the evils associated with
illicit drugs are either exaggerated or misapplied effects not of
the drugs, but of the government's prohibition of them.

More to the point, none of this is working, even taking
drug war advocates' positions at face value. It is as easy to
achieve an illegal high today as it was in 1981, as it was in
1971, as it was in 1915. The vast majority of you reading this
either know where to get a bag of marijuana, or know someone who knows where to get one. Specific drugs come in and
out of vogue, but the desire to alter one's consciousness, to escape life's drab monotonies, or just to call in a different mindset is as strong and pervasive as it's ever been, going back to
the stone age. It's also just as easy to fulfill.

In a 1986 speech designed to drum up public support for
yet another round of War on Drugs legislation, President
Ronald Reagan officially designated illicit drugs a threat to
America's national security. After declaring that, "We're running up a battle flag," Reagan then compared America's determination in the war on drugs to that of the French troops at
the World War I Battle of Verdun. As the journalist Dan Baum
notes while explaining Reagan's speech in his book *Smoke and
Mirrors*, Verdun was a protracted, bloody, brutal battle of at-
trition. A quarter million troops lost their lives and another
700,000 were wounded in the months-long battle for a small
strip of land that offered little practical advantage to either
army. In fact, in much of Europe, Verdun has come to sym-
bolize the futility of war, and the way governments are willing
to write off the mass loss of human life as mere collateral
damage in the pursuit of some seemingly noble but ultimately
shallow and elusive aim.

Looking back, Reagan's analogy was quite a bit more appropriate than he probably intended.

The Global War on Drugs Cannot Be Won

Ethan Nadelmann

Ethan Nadelmann is the founder and executive director of the Drug Policy Alliance, an organization in the United States promoting alternatives to the war on drugs.

A "drug-free world," which the United Nations describes as a realistic goal, is no more attainable than an "alcohol-free world"—and no one has talked about that with a straight face since the repeal of Prohibition in the United States in 1933. Yet futile rhetoric about winning a "war on drugs" persists, despite mountains of evidence documenting its moral and ideological bankruptcy. When the U.N. General Assembly Special Session on drugs convened in 1998, it committed to "eliminating or significantly reducing the illicit cultivation of the coca bush, the cannabis plant and the opium poppy by the year 2008" and to "achieving significant and measurable results in the field of demand reduction." But today, global production and consumption of those drugs are roughly the same as they were a decade ago; meanwhile, many producers have become more efficient, and cocaine and heroin have become purer and cheaper.

It's always dangerous when rhetoric drives policy—and especially so when "war on drugs" rhetoric leads the public to accept collateral casualties that would never be permissible in civilian law enforcement, much less public health. Politicians still talk of eliminating drugs from the Earth as though their use is a plague on humanity. But drug control is not like disease control, for the simple reason that there's no popular demand for smallpox or polio. Cannabis and opium have been grown throughout much of the world for millennia. The same is true for coca in Latin America. Methamphetamine and other synthetic drugs can be produced anywhere. Demand for particular illicit drugs waxes and wanes, depending not just on availability but also fads, fashion, culture, and competition from alternative means of stimulation and distraction. The relative harshness of drug laws and the intensity of enforcement matter surprisingly little, except in totalitarian states. After all, rates of illegal drug use in the United States are the same as, or higher than, Europe, despite America's much more punitive policies. . . .

The relative harshness of drug laws and the intensity of enforcement matter surprisingly little, except in totalitarian states.

The Demand for Drugs

Reducing the demand for illegal drugs seems to make sense. But the desire to alter one's state of consciousness, and to use psychoactive drugs to do so, is nearly universal—and mostly not a problem. There's virtually never been a drug-free society, and more drugs are discovered and devised every year. Demand-reduction efforts that rely on honest education and positive alternatives to drug use are helpful, but not when they devolve into unrealistic, "zero tolerance" policies.

As with sex, abstinence from drugs is the best way to avoid trouble, but one always needs a fallback strategy for those who can't or won't refrain. "Zero tolerance" policies deter some people, but they also dramatically increase the harms and costs for those who don't resist. Drugs become more potent, drug use becomes more hazardous, and people who use drugs are marginalized in ways that serve no one.

The better approach is not demand reduction but "harm reduction." Reducing drug use is fine, but it's not nearly as important as reducing the death, disease, crime, and suffering associated with both drug misuse and failed prohibitionist policies. With respect to legal drugs, such as alcohol and cigarettes, harm reduction means promoting responsible drinking and designated drivers, or persuading people to switch to nicotine patches, chewing gums, and smokeless tobacco. With respect to illegal drugs, it means reducing the transmission of infectious disease through syringe-exchange programs, reducing overdose fatalities by making antidotes readily available, and allowing people addicted to heroin and other illegal opiates to obtain methadone from doctors and even pharmaceutical heroin from clinics. Britain, Canada, Germany, the Netherlands, and Switzerland have already embraced this last option. There's no longer any question that these strategies decrease drug-related harms without increasing drug use. What blocks expansion of such programs is not cost; they typically save taxpayers' money that would otherwise go to criminal justice and healthcare. No, the roadblocks are abstinence-only ideologues and a cruel indifference to the lives and well-being of people who use drugs. . . .

The carrot and stick of crop eradication and substitution have been tried and failed, with rare exceptions, for half a century.

The Supply of Drugs

Reducing supply makes as much sense as reducing demand; after all, if no one were planting cannabis, coca, and opium, there wouldn't be any heroin, cocaine, or marijuana to sell or consume. But the carrot and stick of crop eradication and substitution have been tried and failed, with rare exceptions, for half a century. These methods may succeed in targeted locales, but they usually simply shift production from one region to another: Opium production moves from Pakistan to Afghanistan; coca from Peru to Colombia; and cannabis from

Mexico to the United States, while overall global production remains relatively constant or even increases.

The carrot, in the form of economic development and assistance in switching to legal crops, is typically both late and inadequate. The stick, often in the form of forced eradication, including aerial spraying, wipes out illegal and legal crops alike and can be hazardous to both people and local environments. The best thing to be said for emphasizing supply reduction is that it provides a rationale for wealthier nations to spend a little money on economic development in poorer countries. But, for the most part, crop eradication and substitution wreak havoc among impoverished farmers without diminishing overall global supply.

The global markets in cannabis, coca, and opium products operate essentially the same way that other global commodity markets do: If one source is compromised due to bad weather, rising production costs, or political difficulties, another emerges. If international drug control circles wanted to think strategically, the key question would no longer be how to reduce global supply, but rather: Where does illicit production cause the fewest problems (and the greatest benefits)? Think of it as a global vice control challenge. No one expects to eradicate vice, but it must be effectively zoned and regulated—even if it's illegal. . . .

Looking to the United States as a role model for drug control is like looking to apartheid-era South Africa for how to deal with race.

U.S. Drug Policy

Looking to the United States as a role model for drug control is like looking to apartheid-era South Africa for how to deal with race. The United States ranks first in the world in per capita incarceration—with less than 5 percent of the world's population, but almost 25 percent of the world's prisoners. The number of people locked up for U.S. drug-law violations has increased from roughly 50,000 in 1980 to almost 500,000 today; that's more than the number of people Western Europe locks up for everything. Even more deadly is U.S. resistance to syringe-exchange programs to reduce HIV/AIDS both at home and abroad. Who knows how many people might not have contracted HIV if the United States had implemented at home, and supported abroad, the sorts of syringe-exchange and other harm-reduction programs that have kept HIV/AIDS rates so low in Australia, Britain, the Netherlands, and elsewhere. Perhaps millions.

And yet, despite this dismal record, the United States has succeeded in constructing an international drug prohibition regime modeled after its own highly punitive and moralistic approach. It has dominated the drug control agencies of the United Nations and other international organizations, and its federal drug enforcement agency was the first national police organization to go global. Rarely has one nation so successfully promoted its own failed policies to the rest of the world.

But now, for the first time, U.S. hegemony in drug control is being challenged. The European Union is demanding rigorous assessment of drug control strategies. Exhausted by decades of service to the U.S.-led war on drugs, Latin Americans are far less inclined to collaborate closely with U.S. drug enforcement efforts. Finally waking up to the deadly threat of HIV/AIDS, China, Indonesia, Vietnam, and even Malaysia and Iran are increasingly accepting of syringe-exchange and other harm-reduction programs. In 2005, the ayatollah in charge of Iran's Ministry of Justice issued a *fatwa* [official decree] declaring methadone maintenance and syringe-exchange programs compatible with *sharia* (Islamic) law. One only wishes his American counterpart were comparably enlightened. . . .

Afghanistan's Opium Production

It's easy to believe that eliminating record-high opium production in Afghanistan—which today accounts for roughly 90 percent of global supply, up from 50 percent 10 years ago—would solve everything from heroin abuse in Europe and Asia to the resurgence of the Taliban.

But assume for a moment that the United States, NATO [North Atlantic Treaty Organization], and [the president of Afghanistan] Hamid Karzai's government were somehow able to cut opium production in Afghanistan. Who would benefit? Only the Taliban, warlords, and other black-market entrepreneurs whose stockpiles of opium would skyrocket in value. Hundreds of thousands of Afghan peasants would flock to cities, ill-prepared to find work. And many Afghans would return to their farms the following year to plant another illegal harvest, utilizing guerrilla farming methods to escape intensified eradication efforts. Except now, they'd soon be competing with poor farmers elsewhere in Central Asia, Latin America, or even Africa. This is, after all, a global commodities market. . . .

Global drug prohibition is clearly a costly disaster.

And outside Afghanistan? Higher heroin prices typically translate into higher crime rates by addicts. They also invite cheaper but more dangerous means of consumption, such as switching from smoking to injecting heroin, which results in higher HIV and Hepatitis C rates. All things considered, wiping out opium in Afghanistan would yield far fewer benefits than is commonly assumed.

So what's the solution? Some recommend buying up all the opium in Afghanistan, which would cost a lot less than is now being spent trying to eradicate it. But, given that farmers somewhere will produce opium so long as the demand for heroin persists, maybe the world is better off, all things considered, with 90 percent of it coming from just one country. And if that heresy becomes the new gospel, it opens up all sorts of possibilities for pursuing a new policy in Afghanistan that reconciles the interests of the United States, NATO, and millions of Afghan citizens.

The Legalization of Drugs

Global drug prohibition is clearly a costly disaster. The United Nations has estimated the value of the global market in illicit drugs at $400 billion, or 6 percent of global trade. The extraordinary profits available to those willing to assume the risks enrich criminals, terrorists, violent political insurgents, and corrupt politicians and governments. Many cities, states, and even countries in Latin America, the Caribbean, and Asia are reminiscent of Chicago under [Prohibition era gangster] Al Capone—times 50. By bringing the market for drugs out into the open, legalization would radically change all that for the better.

More importantly, legalization would strip addiction down to what it really is: a health issue. Most people who use drugs are like the responsible alcohol consumer, causing no harm to themselves or anyone else. They would no longer be the state's business. But legalization would also benefit those who struggle with drugs by reducing the risks of overdose and disease associated with unregulated products, eliminating the need to obtain drugs from dangerous criminal markets, and allowing addiction problems to be treated as medical rather than criminal problems.

No one knows how much governments spend collectively on failing drug war policies, but it's probably at least $100 billion a year, with federal, state, and local governments in the United States accounting for almost half the total. Add to that the tens of billions of dollars to be gained annually in tax revenues from the sale of legalized drugs. Now imagine if just a third of that total were committed to reducing drug-related disease and addiction. Virtually everyone, except those who profit or gain politically from the current system, would benefit.

Some say legalization is immoral. That's nonsense, unless one believes there is some principled basis for discriminating against people based solely on what they put into their bodies, absent harm to others. Others say legalization would open the floodgates to huge increases in drug abuse. They forget that we already live in a world in which psychoactive drugs of all sorts are readily available—and in which people too poor to buy drugs resort to sniffing gasoline, glue, and other industrial products, which can be more harmful than any drug. No, the greatest downside to legalization may well be the fact that the legal markets would fall into the hands of the powerful alcohol, tobacco, and pharmaceutical companies. Still, legalization is a far more pragmatic option than living with the corruption, violence, and organized crime of the current system. . . .

Partial Legalization

Wholesale legalization may be a long way off—but partial legalization is not. If any drug stands a chance of being legalized, it's cannabis [marijuana]. Hundreds of millions of people have used it, the vast majority without suffering any harm or going on to use "harder" drugs. In Switzerland, for example, cannabis legalization was twice approved by one chamber of its parliament, but narrowly rejected by the other.

Elsewhere in Europe, support for the criminalization of cannabis is waning. In the United States, where roughly 40 percent of the country's 1.8 million annual drug arrests are for cannabis possession, typically of tiny amounts, 40 percent of Americans say that the drug should be taxed, controlled, and regulated like alcohol. Encouraged by Bolivian President Evo Morales, support is also growing in Latin America and Europe for removing coca from international antidrug conventions, given the absence of any credible health reason for keeping it there. Traditional growers would benefit economically, and there's some possibility that such products might compete favorably with more problematic substances, including alcohol.

The global war on drugs persists in part because so many people fail to distinguish between the harms of drug abuse and the harms of prohibition. Legalization forces that distinction to the forefront. The opium problem in Afghanistan is primarily a prohibition problem, not a drug problem. The same is true of the narcoviolence and corruption that has afflicted Latin America and the Caribbean for almost three decades—and that now threatens Africa. Governments can arrest and kill drug lord after drug lord, but the ultimate solution is a structural one, not a prosecutorial one. Few people doubt any longer that the war on drugs is lost, but courage and vision are needed to transcend the ignorance, fear, and vested interests that sustain it.

The War on Drugs Leads to Violence

John McWhorter

John McWhorter is a conservatice political commentator, a se-
nior fellow at the Manhattan Institute, and a lecturer at Colum-
bia University in linguistics.

It's one of those hideous little episodes making minor headlines this week [in November 2009] that will be forgotten
by the media next week. 15-year-old Vada Vasquez of the
Bronx is in a coma with a bullet in her brain, after being
caught in the crossfire when a group of Bloods [a violent
gang] took aim at 19-year-old Tyrone Creighton (and succeeding; he's in the hospital, too).

The Drug Turf

The Bloods went after Creighton at the behest of friends of a
man in Rikers [New York City prison] who suffered a beat-
down by Creighton's two brothers in Rikers with him. The
shooter was allegedly little 16-year-old Carvett Gentles, "baby-
faced," as the stories are terming him with the regularity of a
Homeric [after the ancient Greek poet Homer] epithet.

Tuesday night [November 17, 2009,] there was a vigil for
Vasquez, the usual scene with the usual "Stop The Violence"
placards. This is the kind of event about which wise heads
regularly intone about how the problem is with family disci-
pline, with inadequate schools, with inadequate community
policing, with the availability of guns.

All true. But there is another *primum mobile* [first mover]
in this case, as is also usual: drugs. Creighton's brothers are in
[prison] for killing a Bronx man three years ago—and it is

John McWhorter, "Murder in the Bronx, Business as Usual: A Suggestion for Obama in
2014," *The New Republic*, November 19, 2009. Copyright © 2009 by The New Republic,
Inc. Reproduced by permission of The New Republic.

doubtful that they did it simply for sport because there were no deer around to shoot. Ghetto murders of this kind are typically connected with maintaining turf in the sale of drugs. Plus, the Bloods are not exactly uninvolved with selling drugs, and Gentles was the only one of his group without a criminal record. And Tyrone Creighton himself has been out on bail for attempted murder and drug charges.

There is good money to be made by selling drugs on the street, because they are illegal and prosecuted, driving up the profit margin. And that means that, details aside, we can all agree that what happened in the Bronx on Monday would have been very different if there were no War on Drugs. In fact, it probably wouldn't have happened at all.

The simple fact is that if there were no profit to be made in selling drugs on the street, no one would bother.

The War on Drugs

It's one more indication of what a tragedy this modern replay of the disaster of the Volstead Act [of 1919 which prohibited alcohol in the United States] currently is. The simple fact is that if there were no profit to be made in selling drugs on the street, no one would bother. For all of the "root causes" reasons so many young black and Latino men turn to this trade instead of seeking legal work, if there were no War on Drugs, they would seek other solutions to the obstacles that face them. And whatever those were, they would involve less murder, fewer crossfire injuries and killings of the kind that have likely ruined Ms. Vasquez' life at 15, fewer men in prison for long periods, and fewer of their children growing up fatherless and on their way to repeating their fathers' mistakes.

I am moved in the light of this by the recent policy paper by the Transform Drug Policy Foundation, carefully outlining what a world could be like without a War on Drugs, where instead, even hard drugs are treated as controlled substances.

Yes: heroin by prescription. It sounds weird and menacing now, but so, once, did injecting people with viruses as vaccines. To someone who was born in the teens or early twenties [of the twentieth century], it looked strangely libertine when the sale of alcohol was reinstated—they had never known anything else.

Just as today, ever fewer of us have vivid memory of a time when selling drugs was not yet a common lifestyle choice among disadvantaged men, for the simple reason that there was no nationwide regime devoted to "stamping out" drug use and driving up the profit to be made in selling them underground.

A Proposal for Legalized Drugs

The new report lays it down straight:

> We recommend making drugs available in standard units, with the base unit for each drug carefully calculated on a case by case basis. The riskier the product, the more limited access should be. Illicit diversion into secondary markets could be mitigated through the use of microtaggants, ensuring full traceability of all drugs thus supplied.

Remember: the motivation here is not some kind of Timothy Leary-esque libertinism [Leary, a Harvard psychologist, was a proponent of psychadelic drug benefits]. The primary reason for trying this is to eliminate the incentive to sell drugs illegally, which, under current conditions, is a logical calculus despite the risks connected with it:

> Illicit drug traders are strongly motivated by the huge profit margins available to them. Simultaneously undercutting their prices, and providing more reliable products, will have a substantial negative impact on the viability of their businesses as a whole.

What we need is a kind of imagination:

> An injecting heroin user under a more stringent prohibition regime might be funding a "street" heroin habit with prostitution and property crime, using adulterated drugs in unsafe environments, supplied by a criminal trafficking/dealing infrastructure that can be traced back to illicit sources in Afghanistan. An equivalent user under a regulated regime would be using legally manufactured and prescribed heroin in a supervised clinical setting, thus obviating any need for, or support of, criminal behaviors or organizations.

Prohibition Is Outdated

The report is pure common sense. Any quibbles you have about advertising (there wouldn't be any), use by minors (ditto), whether drugs should be sold near schools (guess!), whether the new regime would include rehabilitation (ditto), and what we would do about the loss of income to countries like Afghanistan dependent on illegal drug sales (NGOs [nongovernmental organizations] and academics, get to work) are answered in it. Including: the program would be introduced in steps—pot [marijuana] first, check how that goes (and the chances it wouldn't go just fine are minuscule), and then move on to the harder stuff.

Our "War on Drugs" is beginning to be yet one more way we look antediluvian to other countries.

In the future, the America of our times will look antediluvian [pre-Flood; i.e., very outdated] for considering this a risky proposition. Jack Cole, head of Law Enforcement Against Prohibition whom I blogged a bit about a little while back has an apt blurb for the book-length report: "In years to come we'll look back at prohibition, and the only question we'll ask is why it lasted so long."

Or, never mind the future: our "War on Drugs" is beginning to be yet one more way we look antediluvian to other countries. Portugal stopped prosecuting drug possession in 2001, and since then there has been no increase in use—and an increase in those seeking rehab. Spain, Italy, the Czech Republic, Estonia, Latvia, and parts of Germany and Switzerland have also stopped prosecuting for possession—and the sky isn't falling yet.

A Reasonable Alternative

Is it that employment opportunities for poor minority men are so very sparse that selling drugs is their only choice? On that, I have always been struck by a weak spot in [anthropologist] Katherine Newman's diligent minor classic *No Shame in My Game*, in which she tries to make that kind of point but has to acknowledge that within families, there are people who go the wrong way but others who do okay. "We have no compelling explanations of why the same family produces such divergent pathways in life," she writes—but the thing is, this does happen, and constantly. One guy sells drugs and goes to jail while his brother is a security guard and his cousin installs cable.

Negative role modelling is clearly a major issue. Tyrone Creighton's life path so far, for example, likely has something to do with what he grew up seeing his older brothers now in Rikers doing—it's all he knew. In a context where quick money is available selling drugs, a Zeitgeist ["spirit of the times"; i.e., a culture] even sets in that legal work is a vanilla, submissive copout, "chump change"—Newman describes ghetto teens mocking peers for working:

> To go there and work for Burger Barn, that was one of those real cloak-and-dagger kinds of things. You'll be coming out—"Yo, where you going?" You be, "I'm going, don't worry about where I'm going." And you see your friends coming and see you working there and now you be, "No, the whole Project gonna know I work in Burger Barn." It's not something I personally proclaim with pride and stuff.

Or, think about the scene in [television show] *The Wire* when Stringer Bell, head of the Barksdale gang, wants to smoke out a snitch. His strategy is to hold back payments for a while and see which person doesn't complain—because that person must be getting cash from some other source for informing. As to the others, "What are they gonna do, go get a job???" he asks in jocular fashion. But crucially, Stringer doesn't mean that they couldn't—as we see when in a late episode in the series Poot leaves gangbanging and gets a job selling shoes. Not glamorous but it's something—a start.

Tyrone Creighton's brothers would have done the same kind of thing in a world where a crazy and futile War on Drugs didn't present them with a *reasonable* alternative, with an air of normalcy in a neighborhood where they grow up watching peers make the same choice.

An Urgent Mission

The Congressional Black Caucus of late have decided to concentrate on health care and employment in their advocacy for the black community, which is all well and good, but it would seem that young black men would be best poised to take full advantage of the latter in an America in which there was no shady but tempting alternate choice of work ever looming.

And between that and the endless procession of scenes like the recent one in the Bronx—lately, several in Chicago, for example, including ones (gang-related) over the past few days—I find myself wishing the [Barack] Obama Administration would take yet one more thing on its plate as an urgent mission in a new America, the War on Drugs.

Not now, I know. Drug policy czar Gil Kerlikowske has harrumphed: "It is not something the President and I discuss; it isn't even on the agenda." He goes on that "legalized, regulated drugs are not a panacea—pharmaceutical drugs are tightly regulated and government controlled, yet we know they cause untold damage to those who abuse them."

Surely this isn't what Kerlikowske or Obama think in private, turning a blind eye to the larger harms that the War on Drugs creates. Clearly, they have decided the nation has other priorities at present, and the brutal truth is that they are right. As hideous as what happened to Vada Vasquez is—as well as to Tyrone Creighton, not only in the bullet he took but in the kind of occupation he drank in as a norm rather than as a fate to be avoided like kryptonite—perhaps the unemployment crisis, the real estate crisis, the health care crisis, and even global warming are more urgent matters in the grand scheme of things just now.

The War on Drugs stands as an obstacle to people becoming the best that they can be.

An Un-American Obstacle

Now, that is. However, how about in 2014, when Obama has just two years to go and other things are presumably taken care of to the extent that they can be (and assuming that [Republican senator from South Dakota] John Thune, [governor of Minnesota] Tim Pawlenty and [2008 vice presidential candidate] Sarah Palin will not turn out to be the GOP's [Republican Party's] secret weapons three years from now [in 2012])? By then Obama will not be facing re-election, nor will he likely be mired in a sex scandal [as was President Bill Clinton] to distract him from real work.

For now, maybe we have to face things like what happened in the Bronx Monday as a weekly kind of event. But what kind of a nation are we to treat episodes like that one as business as usual? The War on Drugs stands as an obstacle to people becoming the best that they can be. It is, in its way, un-American.

And how can we consider ourselves a country of any serious intellectual or moral advancement to suppose that a constructive response is to settle for idle recitations about "stopping the violence," utopian notions that we could keep guns out of the hands of people whose livelihoods depend on them, and empty calls for strong parenting?

CHAPTER 2

Should U.S. Drug Policy Be Reformed?

Overview: U.S. Federal Drug Policy

Celinda Franco

Celinda Franco is a specialist in crime policy for the Congressional Research Service, a think tank that provides reports to members of Congress.

Current federal domestic drug enforcement efforts are rooted in a long history of legislation that spans most of the past century. Early federal drug control laws established the objective of suppressing the nonmedical use of narcotic drugs, a classification that originally included only opium and its derivatives morphine and heroin, although soon after also encompassed cocaine. The Narcotics Act of 1914, commonly known as the Harrison Narcotics Act, is generally considered the first federal drug control statute. It established the basis for current drug enforcement policy by criminalizing the manufacture, sale, possession, and nonmedical use of narcotics. The law regulated the importation, manufacture, and distribution of opium and coca derivatives, and required legitimate dealers in narcotics to register with the federal government and pay a special annual tax. Under the law, Congress acted to protect public safety and health by establishing labeling requirements for medicines and other substances that were legally available, although not previously subject to federal regulation. The law instituted limitations on certain aspects of accepted physician and pharmaceutical practices related to the medical use of narcotic substances. In addition to instituting various regulatory and control mechanisms, the law established mechanisms for enforcing federal criminal penalties for violations of these provisions.

Celinda Franco, "Federal Domestic Illegal Drug Enforcement Efforts: Are They Working?" Washington, DC: Congressional Research Service: CRS Report for Congress, 2009.

Federal Drug Control Laws

Generally, Congress has taken a "prohibitory approach" to drugs considered to be threats to the general public welfare by establishing criminal penalties aimed at dissuading and deterring illegal suppliers and consumers of controlled substances. Federal drug control policy has also been shaped by shifting social and cultural currents, as well as by changing trends in drug use and societal tolerance of such use. For example, early drug control laws (i.e., the Marijuana Tax Act of 1937) targeted specific drug problems as their use became a public safety concern. This led to a patchwork of federal statutes that imposed drug-specific criminal penalties that became increasingly stringent. Although early federal anti-drug strategy relied on punitive measures to address the illegal drug problem, the scale of illegal drug use and federal involvement in drug enforcement were relatively minor until the end of the 1960s.

The scale of illegal drug use and federal involvement in drug enforcement were relatively minor until the end of the 1960s.

In 1970, the Controlled Substances Act (CSA) was enacted as Title II of the Comprehensive Drug Abuse Prevention and Control Act of 1970. Congress passed the CSA to clarify the federal role in the control of dangerous drugs, chemicals, and substances, replacing and consolidating prior disparate federal drug laws. Among other provisions, Title II of the CSA established five "schedules" for various drugs, plants, psychoactive substances, and chemicals, ranking them "by a common standard of dangerousness," and balancing the potential for abuse against their medical usefulness by applying differing degrees of control on manufacturers, distributors, and prescribing physicians. The CSA provided federal criminal penalties for the illegal manufacture, distribution, and possession of controlled substances. The law also established the framework for regulating the importation, exportation, and manufacture of controlled substances through registration requirements and penalties for violation of these provisions.

Today, the CSA, as amended, continues to provide the legal framework for federal drug control and enforcement activities. The numerous provisions of the CSA regulate the use of controlled substances for legitimate medical, scientific, research, and industrial purposes and make the diversion of these substances illegal. Over the years, Congress has amended the CSA a number of times to reflect changes in the patterns of drug abuse, the development of new psychoactive substances, and to change the related federal penalties. Questions have been raised, however, about whether these and other fundamental tenets of federal drug enforcement policy form an effective strategy.

Federal drug enforcement policy ... is based on the premise that drug use can be reduced if the availability, or supply, of illegal drugs is curbed or eliminated.

Federal Drug Enforcement

Federal drug enforcement policy, as one of the three components of the national drug control strategy, is based on the premise that drug use can be reduced if the availability, or supply, of illegal drugs is curbed or eliminated. As such, federal domestic drug enforcement activities consist of two overarching methods: (1) domestic law enforcement efforts designed to disrupt all levels of the illicit drug distribution chain to keep illegal drugs from reaching domestic retail markets and drug users through investigations, arrests, seizures of illegal drugs, prosecutions, incarceration, the seizure and forfeiture of drug-related assets and monies, and fines; and (2) interdiction, or the interception of illegal drug shipments in transit to the United States either across U.S. waters or across land borders. These tactics focus on limiting the supply of illegal drugs to make it more difficult, costly, and risky to traffic in, distribute, sell, use or abuse illegal substances.

Several federal agencies play key roles in implementing domestic enforcement activities. The Department of Justice (DOJ) is the federal agency responsible for enforcing federal criminal laws, and a number of its agencies and divisions play key roles in enforcing anti-drug laws by investigating, arresting, prosecuting, and incarcerating federal drug offenders. At DOJ, the Drug Enforcement Administration (DEA) is the only federal agency whose sole mission is to enforce federal drug laws. Some aspects of DEA's role include

- conducting investigations and preparing for the prosecutions of major drug offenders;

- seizing assets derived from, traceable to, or intended to be used for illegal drug trafficking;

- managing the El Paso Intelligence Center, a multi-agency drug intelligence program designed to collect, analyze, and disseminate strategic and operational drug intelligence information to assist federal, state, local, and foreign law enforcement efforts to counter drug, alien, and weapons smuggling;

- conducting a money laundering program, in conjunction with the U.S. Department of Treasury, to investigate, track, and disrupt the movement of illegal drug proceeds used to fund continued operations of drug trafficking organizations; and

- coordinating task forces of other federal, state, and local law enforcement agencies on drug enforcement efforts to enhance potential interstate investigations beyond local or limited federal jurisdictions with combined resources.

Several other DOJ agencies with general crime-fighting missions also play an important part in domestic anti-drug activities, including the Federal Bureau of Investigation (FBI); Executive Office for U.S. Attorneys (EOUSA); the Bureau of Alcohol, Tobacco, Firearms and Explosives (ATF); and the U.S. Marshals Service (USMS). DOJ's Organized Crime Drug Enforcement Task Force (OCDETF) program combines federal law enforcement resources with those of state and local law enforcement to identify and disrupt drug trafficking and money laundering organizations. The National Drug Intelligence Center (NDIC), a separate component of DOJ, coordinates and consolidates drug intelligence from all national security and law enforcement agencies to provide strategic drug-related intelligence to assist with drug control efforts. In addition, Department of Homeland Security (DHS) agencies, including the U.S. Customs and Border Protection (CBP), U.S. Coast Guard (USCG), and Immigration and Customs Enforcement (ICE), are involved in the apprehension of drug smugglers and the interdiction of illegal drugs. The Office of Counternarcotics Enforcement (CNE) is charged with coordinating policy and efforts to interdict illegal drug trafficking at DHS.

The Office of National Drug Control Policy (ONDCP) is the lead federal agency tasked with organizing and overseeing federal drug control efforts. ONDCP annually issues a report on the national drug control strategy and provides estimates of the federal drug control budget. ONDCP also funds drug enforcement efforts through the High Intensity Drug Trafficking Areas (HIDTA) program. Currently, 28 HIDTAs provide additional federal resources for state and local law enforcement agencies in areas of the country designated as having serious drug trafficking problems to assist with coordination efforts, equipment, and technology. Under the HIDTA program, federal support is provided to 45 states, Puerto Rico, the U.S. Virgin Islands, and the District of Columbia. . . .

The Debate About Drug Policy

For more than 30 years Congress has responded to the illegal drug problem at the federal level with enforcement measures aimed at drug-supply reduction measures as a means of curbing illegal drug use. At the federal level, more than 323,000 drug arrests were made between 1998 and 2007, and many of these defendants were charged with trafficking or drug distribution offenses. Over this period, 258,204 federal drug offenders were convicted. In September 2008, there were almost 100,000 inmates in federal prisons convicted and sentenced for drug offenses, representing more than 52% of all federal prisoners. Federal spending for domestic drug enforcement and interdiction efforts between FY [fiscal year] 1998 and FY 2008 exceeded $58.8 billion, representing more than 82% of total federal funding for all supply-reduction efforts, and more than 58% of total federal spending for all drug control efforts for those years. Additionally, ONDCP estimates that the cost of incarcerating federal drug offenders in FY 2008 exceeded $2.9 billion.

There is little agreement on how to best address the drug problem, and the merits of federal drug enforcement efforts are at the heart of the debate.

Federal drug enforcement efforts are an important aspect of national drug control policy. Yet, there is little agreement on how to best address the drug problem, and the merits of federal drug enforcement efforts are at the heart of the debate. Some argue that the emphasis on drug enforcement is not an effective strategy. Others argue that these efforts are not optimally balanced with other drug control strategies, such as reducing the demand for illegal drugs. Some are of the opinion that what is required to stop illegal drug use and distribution are more punitive sanctions and more emphasis on enforcement. Still others have suggested that existing drug enforcement efforts should be considered a success as long as drug use does not continue to increase. While such divergent views on drug control policy are difficult to reconcile, better information on drug enforcement efforts might help to focus and inform the debate.

Despite federal efforts to reduce the supply and use of illegal drugs, illegal drugs remain a persistent social problem in the United States. It has been noted that federal drug control policy has not fundamentally changed since the mid-1980s, despite significant shifts in the nature of the illegal drug problem. However, empirical assessments of federal enforcement efforts are hampered by the lack of data and research. Research could provide a better understanding of how federal law enforcement efforts support the objectives of drug control policy and inform the future development of more effective enforcement strategies.

The United States Should Repeal Federal Drug Prohibition

David Boaz and Timothy Lynch

David Boaz is the executive vice president of the Cato Institute, a nonprofit public policy research foundation, and author of The Politics of Freedom: Taking on The Left, The Right, and Threats to Our Liberties. *Timothy Lynch is the director of the Project on Criminal Justice at the Cato Institute and author of* After Prohibition: An Adult Approach to Drug Policies in the 21st Century.

Ours is a federal republic. The federal government has only the powers granted to it in the Constitution. And the United States has a tradition of individual liberty, vigorous civil society, and limited government. Identification of a problem does not mean that the government should undertake to solve it, and the fact that a problem occurs in more than one state does not mean that it is a proper subject for federal policy.

The Prohibition of Drugs

Perhaps no area more clearly demonstrates the bad consequences of not following such rules than does drug prohibition. The long federal experiment in prohibition of marijuana, cocaine, heroin, and other drugs has given us crime and corruption combined with a manifest failure to stop the use of drugs or reduce their availability to children.

In the 1920s, Congress experimented with the prohibition of alcohol. On February 20, 1933, a new Congress acknowledged the failure of alcohol prohibition and sent the Twenty-First Amendment to the states. Congress recognized that Prohibition had failed to stop drinking and had increased prison populations and violent crime. By the end of 1933, national Prohibition was history, though many states continued to outlaw or severely restrict the sale of liquor.

Today, Congress confronts a similarly failed prohibition policy. Futile efforts to enforce prohibition have been pursued even more vigorously since the 1980s than they were in the 1920s. Total federal expenditures for the first 10 years of Prohibition amounted to $88 million—about $1 billion in 2008 dollars. Drug enforcement costs about $19 billion a year now in federal spending alone.

Those billions have had some effect. Total drug arrests are now more than 1.5 million a year. Since 1989, more people have been incarcerated for drug offenses than for all violent crimes combined. There are now about 480,000 drug offenders in jails and prisons, and about 50 percent of the federal prison population consists of drug offenders.

All the arrests and incarcerations haven't stopped the use and abuse of drugs, or the drug trade, or the crime associated with black-market transactions.

The Failure of Drug Prohibition

Yet, as was the case during Prohibition, all the arrests and incarcerations haven't stopped the use and abuse of drugs, or the drug trade, or the crime associated with black-market transactions. Cocaine and heroin supplies are up; the more our Customs agents interdict, the more smugglers import. And most tragic, the crime rate has soared. Despite the good news about crime in recent years, crime rates remain at high levels.

As for discouraging young people from using drugs, the massive federal effort has largely been a dud. Every year from 1975 to 2006, at least 82 percent of high school seniors said they found marijuana "fairly easy" or "very easy" to obtain. During that same period, according to federal statistics of dubious reliability, teenage marijuana use fell dramatically and then rose significantly, suggesting that cultural factors have more effect than the "war on drugs."

The manifest failure of drug prohibition explains why more and more political leaders, such as [now former] Governors Jesse Ventura [of Minnesota] and Gary Johnson [of New Mexico] and Rep. Barney Frank (D-MA), have argued that drug prohibition actually causes more crime and other harms than it prevents. Senator Jim Webb (D-VA) has also been outspoken in his criticism of federal drug policies. In his 2008 book, *A Time to Fight*, Webb wrote: "Drug addiction is not in and of itself a criminal act. It is a medical condition, indeed a disease, just as alcoholism is, and we don't lock people up for being alcoholics."

The Controlled Substances Act

The United States is a federal republic, and Congress should deal with drug prohibition the way it dealt with alcohol prohibition. The Twenty-First Amendment did not actually legalize the sale of alcohol; it simply repealed the federal prohibition and returned to the several states the authority to set alcohol policy. States took the opportunity to design diverse liquor policies that were in tune with the preferences of their citizens. After 1933, three states and hundreds of counties continued to practice prohibition. Other states chose various forms of alcohol legalization.

The single most important law that Congress must repeal is the Controlled Substances Act of 1970. That law is probably the most far-reaching federal statute in American history, since it asserts federal jurisdiction over every drug offense in the United States, no matter how small or local in scope. Once that law is removed from the statute books, Congress should move to abolish the Drug Enforcement Administration [DEA] and repeal all the other federal drug laws.

There are a number of reasons why Congress should end the federal government's war on drugs. First and foremost, the federal drug laws are constitutionally dubious. As previously noted, the federal government can exercise only the powers that have been delegated to it. The Tenth Amendment reserves all other powers to the states or to the people. However misguided the alcohol prohibitionists turned out to have been, they deserve credit for honoring our constitutional system by seeking a constitutional amendment that would explicitly authorize a national policy on the sale of alcohol. Congress never asked the American people for additional constitutional powers to declare a war on drug consumers. That usurpation of power is something that few politicians or their court intellectuals wish to discuss.

Addicts commit crimes to pay for a habit that would be easily affordable if it were legal.

Drugs and Crime

Second, drug prohibition creates high levels of crime. Addicts commit crimes to pay for a habit that would be easily affordable if it were legal. Police sources have estimated that as much as half the property crime in some major cities is committed by drug users. More dramatically, because drugs are illegal, participants in the drug trade cannot go to court to settle disputes, whether between buyer and seller or between rival sellers. When black-market contracts are breached, the result is often some form of violent sanction, which usually leads to retaliation and then open warfare in the streets.

Our capital city, Washington, D.C., became known as the "murder capital" even though it is the most heavily policed city in the United States. Make no mistake about it, the annual carnage that accounts for America's still high murder rates has little to do with the mind-altering effects of a marijuana cigarette or a crack pipe. It is instead one of the grim and bitter consequences of an ideological crusade whose proponents will not yet admit defeat.

Third, since the calamity of September 11, 2001, U.S. intelligence officials have repeatedly warned us of further terrorist attacks. Given that danger, it is a gross misallocation of law enforcement resources to have federal police agents surveilling marijuana clubs in California when they could be helping to discover sleeper cells of terrorists on U.S. territory. The Drug Enforcement Administration has 10,000 agents, intelligence analysts, and support staff members. Their skills would be much better used if those people were redeployed to full-time counterterrorism investigations.

Drugs and Money

Fourth, drug prohibition is a classic example of throwing money at a problem. The federal government spends some $19 billion to enforce the drug laws every year—all to no avail. For years, drug war bureaucrats have been tailoring their budget requests to the latest news reports. When drug use goes up, taxpayers are told the government needs more money so that it can redouble its efforts against a rising drug scourge. When drug use goes down, taxpayers are told that it would be a big mistake to curtail spending just when progress is being made. Good news or bad, spending levels must be maintained or increased.

Fifth, drug prohibition channels more than $40 billion a year into a criminal underworld that is occupied by an assortment of criminals, corrupt politicians, and, yes, terrorists. Alcohol prohibition drove reputable companies into other industries or out of business altogether, which paved the way for mobsters to make millions in the black market. If drugs were legal, organized crime would stand to lose billions of dollars, and drugs would be sold by legitimate businesses in an open marketplace.

Drug prohibition has created a criminal subculture in our inner cities. The immense profits to be had from a black-market business make drug dealing the most lucrative endeavor for many people, especially those who care least about getting on the wrong side of the law.

A Social Failure

Drug dealers become the most visibly successful people in inner-city communities, the ones with money and clothes and cars. Social order is turned upside down when the most successful people in a community are criminals. The drug war makes peace and prosperity virtually impossible in inner cities.

The failures of drug prohibition are becoming obvious to more and more Americans.

Students of American history will someday ponder the question of how today's elected officials could readily admit to the mistaken policy of alcohol prohibition in the 1920s but recklessly pursue a policy of drug prohibition. Indeed, the only historical lesson that recent presidents and Congresses seem to have drawn from Prohibition is that government should not try to outlaw the sale of booze. One of the broader lessons that they should have learned is this: prohibition laws should be judged according to their real-world effects, not their promised benefits. If the [current] Congress will subject the federal drug laws to that standard, it will recognize that the drug war is not the answer to problems associated with drug use.

Medical Marijuana

The failures of drug prohibition are becoming obvious to more and more Americans. A particularly tragic consequence of the stepped-up war on drugs is the refusal to allow sick people to use marijuana as medicine. Prohibitionists insist that marijuana is not good medicine, or at least that there are legal alternatives to marijuana that are equally good. Those who believe that individuals should make their own decisions, not have their decisions made for them by Washington bureaucracies, would simply say that that's a decision for patients and their doctors to make. But in fact there is good medical evidence of the therapeutic value of marijuana— despite the difficulty of doing adequate research on an illegal drug. A National Institutes of Health panel concluded that smoking marijuana may help treat a number of conditions, including nausea and pain. It can be particularly effective in improving the appetite of AIDS and cancer patients. The drug could also assist people who fail to respond to traditional remedies.

More than 70 percent of U.S. cancer specialists in one survey said they would prescribe marijuana if it were legal; nearly half said they had urged their patients to break the law to acquire the drug. The British Medical Association reports that nearly 70 percent of its members believe marijuana should be available for therapeutic use. Even President George Bush's Office of National Drug Control Policy criticized the Department of Health and Human Services for closing its special medical marijuana program.

Respect for State Initiatives

Whatever the actual value of medical marijuana, the relevant fact for federal policymakers is that 12 states have authorized physicians licensed in those states to recommend the use of medical marijuana to seriously ill and terminally ill patients residing in the states, without being subject to civil and criminal penalties.

The Bush administration paid lip service to the importance of federalism, but its actions in Congress and at the state and local levels undermined that principle. Federal police agents and prosecutors continue to raid medical marijuana clubs—especially in California and Arizona. And both of the president's drug policy officials, drug czar John Walters and DEA chief Karen Tandy, used their offices to meddle in state and local politics. If it is inappropriate for governors and mayors to entangle themselves in foreign policy—and it is—it is also inappropriate for federal officials to entangle themselves in state and local politics. In the [preceding] Congress, Reps. Barney Frank (D-MA), Dana Rohrabacher (R-CA), and Ron Paul (R-TX) jointly proposed the States' Rights to Medical Marijuana Act, which would have prohibited federal interference with any state that chose to enact a medical marijuana policy. The [current] Congress should enact a similar bill without delay.

One of the benefits of a federal republic is that different policies may be tried in different states. One of the benefits of our Constitution is that it limits the power of the federal government to impose one policy on the several states.

Repeal Mandatory Minimums

The common law in England and America has always relied on judges and juries to decide cases and set punishments. Under our modern system, of course, many crimes are defined by the legislature, and appropriate penalties are defined by statute. However, mandatory minimum sentences and rigid sentencing guidelines shift too much power to legislators and regulators who are not involved in particular cases. They turn judges into clerks and prevent judges from weighing all the facts and circumstances in setting appropriate sentences. In addition, mandatory minimums for nonviolent first-time drug offenders result in sentences grotesquely disproportionate to the gravity of the offenses.

Rather than extend mandatory minimum sentences to further crimes, Congress should repeal mandatory minimums and let judges perform their traditional function of weighing the facts and setting appropriate sentences.

The Repeal of Prohibition, Again

Drug abuse is a problem for those involved in it and for their families and friends. But it is better dealt with as a moral and medical problem than as a criminal problem—"a problem for the surgeon general, not the attorney general," as former Baltimore mayor Kurt Schmoke puts it.

The United States is a federal republic, and Congress should deal with drug prohibition the way it dealt with alcohol prohibition. The Twenty-First Amendment did not actually legalize the sale of alcohol; it simply repealed the federal prohibition and returned to the several states the authority to set alcohol policy. States took the opportunity to design diverse liquor policies that were in tune with the preferences of their citizens. After 1933, three states and hundreds of counties continued to practice prohibition. Other states chose various forms of alcohol legalization.

Prohibition has failed, again, and should be repealed, again.

Congress should repeal the Controlled Substances Act of 1970, shut down the Drug Enforcement Administration, and let the states set their own policies with regard to currently illegal drugs. They would do well to treat marijuana, cocaine, and heroin the way most states now treat alcohol: It should be legal for stores to sell such drugs to adults. Drug sales to children, like alcohol sales to children, should remain illegal. Driving under the influence of drugs should be illegal.

With such a policy, Congress would acknowledge that our current drug policies have failed. It would restore authority to the states, as the Founders envisioned. It would save taxpayers' money. And it would give the states the power to experiment with drug policies and perhaps devise more successful rules.

Repeal of prohibition would take the astronomical profits out of the drug business and destroy the drug kingpins who terrorize parts of our cities. It would reduce crime even more dramatically than did the repeal of alcohol prohibition. Not only would there be less crime; reform would also free federal agents to concentrate on terrorism and espionage and free local police agents to concentrate on robbery, burglary, and violent crime.

The war on drugs has lasted longer than Prohibition, longer than the Vietnam War. But there is no light at the end of this tunnel. Prohibition has failed, again, and should be repealed, again.

U.S. Drug Law Enforcement Is Racially Unjust

Human Rights Watch

Human Rights Watch is an independent organization focused on the protection of human rights worldwide.

The punitive anti-drug policies of the last 20 years bear heavy responsibility for the extremely high and disproportionate representation of black Americans in the US prison population.

Drug Offenses and Black Incarceration

Drug offenses have played a greater role in black incarceration than white:

- 38.2 percent of all blacks entering prison in 2003 with new sentences had been convicted of drug offenses, compared to 25.4 percent of whites.

- Between 1990 and 2000, drug offenses accounted for 27 percent of the total increase in black inmates in state prison and only 15 percent of the increase in white inmates.

- Among blacks currently serving state prison sentences, 22.9 percent were convicted of drug offenses; among whites, 14.8 percent.

In some individual states, the impact of drug policies on black incarceration has been far greater: for example, in Illinois, the number of black admissions for drug offenses grew six-fold between 1990 and 2000, while the number of whites admitted for drug offenses remained relatively stable.

Targeting Blacks: Drug Law Enforcement and Race in the United States, New York: Human Rights Watch, 2008. Copyright © 2008 Human Rights Watch. Reproduced by permission.

Racial Disparities

Among the 34 states reporting new admissions to the National Corrections Reporting Program (NCRP) in 2003, there were a total of 111,247 adult men and women who entered state prison that year convicted of drug offenses—possession, sales, manufacturing, or other drug related offenses. The new drug offender prison admissions included 59,535 black men and women (53.5 percent of the total) and 37,003 white men and women (33.3 percent of the total).

Because the proportion of blacks and whites in state populations varies considerably, rates of admission for drug offenses relative to the black and white population of each state present a clearer picture of the racial impact of drug law enforcement than the racial composition of admissions. According to our analysis of the 2003 admissions, ... the total rate of prison admission for blacks in the 34 reporting states was 256.2 per 100,000 adult black residents. For whites, the rate was 25.3 per 100,000 adults. The black rate of admission has grown much faster than the white rate: between 1986 and 2003 the rate of admission to prison for drug offenses for blacks quintupled; the white rate did not quite triple.

In absolute numbers, there are far more whites committing drug offenses than blacks.

The state rates for drug offender prison admissions for whites ranged from a low of 8 (Wisconsin) to a high of 88.3 (Oklahoma) per 100,000 white residents. The rates for drug offender admissions for blacks ranged from a low of 47.5 (Oregon) to a high of 613.8 (Illinois) per 100,000 black residents. The five states with the highest black drug offender admission rates were Illinois (613.8), South Dakota (526.3), Washington (449.7), New Jersey (409.4), and Oklahoma (392.4).... In every one of the 34 states, blacks were sent to prison for drug offenses at far higher rates than whites in that state....

Rates of Drug Use

No doubt many Americans believe racial differences in imprisonment for drug offenses reflect racial differences in involvement with illegal drug activities—that blacks are sent to prison at higher rates on drug charges because they are more involved in drug offenses than whites. The heightened media and political attention to substance abuse and the drug trade in urban minority neighborhoods has promoted the public perception that illegal drugs are more prevalent in those neighborhoods than in more affluent white neighborhoods. The reality has long been the reverse. In absolute numbers, there are far more whites committing drug offenses than blacks. The disproportionate rates at which blacks are sent to prison for drug offenses compared to whites largely originate in racially disproportionate rates of arrest for drug offenses.

Use of illegal drugs, by definition, entails the drug offense of illegal possession. The best approximation of comparative rates of drug possession comes from federally-sponsored household surveys of drug use among Americans. Over the years, those surveys have suggested that whites and blacks use illicit drugs at roughly the same rates. For example, according to the most recent survey, an estimated 49 percent of whites and 42.9 percent of blacks age 12 or older have used illicit drugs in their lifetime; 14.5 percent of whites and 16 percent of blacks have used illicit drugs in the past year; and 8.5 percent of whites and 9.8 percent of blacks have used an illicit drug in the past month (those in this latter category are deemed to be current drug users).

Because the white population in the United States is slightly more than six times larger than the black population, and the rate of drug use is roughly comparable between the two, the number of white drug users is significantly higher than the number who are black. For example, according to the 2006 surveys conducted by the federal Substance Abuse and Mental Health Services Administration (SAMHSA), an estimated 111,774,000 people in the United States age 12 or older have used illicit drugs during their lifetime, of whom 82,587,000 are white and 12,477,000 are black. There are also far more whites than blacks among people who have used cocaine in any form in their lifetime, as well as among those who have used crack cocaine. According to the 2006 SAMHSA estimates, there are 27,083,000 whites who have used cocaine during their lifetime, compared to 2,618,000 blacks, and 5,553,000 whites who have used crack cocaine, compared to 1,536,000 blacks. If black and white drug users are combined (and leaving aside other races), blacks account for 13 percent of the total who—according to SAMSHA surveys—have ever used an illicit drug, 8 percent of those who have ever used cocaine, and 21 percent of those who have ever used crack cocaine.

Demographics of Drug Sellers

There is relatively little research on the demographics of drug sellers as such. Little is known about the racial composition of drug kingpins and major traffickers, but . . . it is those at the bottom of the drug trade—for example, those engaging in direct transactions with drug users—who constitute most of the drug sellers who enter the criminal justice system and ultimately prison. Such data as is available suggests, however, that low-level drug sellers have a similar racial profile to drug users. In addition to the illegal activity of drug possession, drug users typically engage in the activities of transferring, selling, and distributing drugs to friends, acquaintances, or strangers. Such activities are illegal in all states even when the transferring activities are not connected to compensation—for example, when someone makes a collective purchase to divide among friends. If the preponderance of drug users are white, then a preponderance of those who transfer or sell to another user are probably also white.

There is research suggesting people typically obtain their drugs from persons of their own race. For example, drug users questioned in a study of patterns of drug purchase and use in six major cities consistently reported that their main drug sources were sellers of the same racial or ethnic background as themselves. As one researcher addressing racial congruity in drug activities concluded, "[D]ealers with direct contact with their customers . . . are likely to look like the customers, and in fact be the customers, at other points in time." Recent research in Seattle's multi-racial and multi-drug drug market indicates that the majority of those who use serious drugs in Seattle are white, as are a majority of the sellers.

The available data, limited as it is, thus suggests that if blacks constitute around 13 percent of the total black and white drug users, they will constitute roughly that proportion of the total black and white drug offenders—those possessing, purchasing, and transferring drugs to others. All other things being equal, they should constitute a roughly similar proportion of people of both races who are arrested, convicted, and sent to prison for drug law violations.

There are numerous factors that help account for drug arrests that are racially disproportionate to drug offending.

Disproportionate Arrest Rates

But all others things are not equal. Blacks constitute 35.1 percent of all drug arrests nationwide. Even if we were to double the 13 percent estimate of the number of blacks who may be drug offenders, the arrest figure is still disproportionately large. Arrest data from some individual states reveal even more dramatic disparities. In Georgia, for example, although blacks constituted approximately 14 percent of all current drug users, they constituted 58 percent of persons arrested for drug possession. Among cocaine users, blacks constituted 22 percent of current users but 79 percent of arrests for cocaine possession. In Illinois blacks accounted for 72 percent of all persons arrested for drug offenses. In Minnesota [according to the Council on Crime and Justice' "Oh, Justice, Where Art Thou?",] "there is a 10:1 disparity in drug-related arrests between African Americans and Whites" that exists despite a study finding a similar level of drug use in Minnesota across racial and ethnic lines. In Wisconsin the rate of black arrests for drug offenses of 2,324 per 100,000 was six times greater than the white rate of 367. In West Virginia non-white males accounted for 26 percent of drug arrests by drug task forces but constituted only 2.5 percent of the state population.

There are numerous factors that help account for drug arrests that are racially disproportionate to drug offending. Of considerable significance is the fact that blacks are more likely to live in cities than whites: according to the US Census Bureau, 51.5 percent of blacks in the US live in a metropolitan area, compared to 21.1 percent of whites. As a general matter, illicit drug use is higher in urban areas, there are more law enforcement resources per capita in urban areas, and there are more drug arrests in urban than in non-urban areas. Drug law enforcement is not, however, evenly distributed within urban areas. Instead, it has focused on low-income, predominantly minority neighborhoods. This is not a "race neutral" factor. Press attention and community concerns about crack cocaine and political imperatives to be "tough on crime" made those neighborhoods the principal "fronts" in the so-called war on drugs. Practical policing factors have played a role as well: drug transactions in poor minority neighborhoods are more likely to be in public spaces and between strangers, making it easier to undertake arrests, such as via "buy and bust" operations, than it is in the bars, clubs, and private homes where drug dealing by whites is more likely to occur. . . .

The absolute number of black drug arrests was dramatically larger in urban areas, as was the percentage of all drug arrestees who were black. There were more than three times as many arrests of blacks in urban areas as in suburban, while there were only 1.7 times as many arrests of whites. These figures also reveal the relatively few arrests that take place in rural areas—only 5 percent of the 1,636,782 drug arrests in 2006 occurred in rural areas. In the 75 largest counties in the United States, blacks in 2002 accounted for 46 percent of drug offense arrests and whites for 29 percent.

Although it is difficult to quantify the extent, racial profiling no doubt plays some role in higher black drug arrests. In Minneapolis, for example, blacks constituted 18 percent of the population but experienced 37 percent of police vehicle stops; whites were 65 percent of the population, but experienced 43 percent of stops. In 1999, 77 percent of young males (ages 18–30) arrested for drug offenses in Minneapolis were black, while 13.8 percent were white. Even when there are dramatic racial disparities in police stops of vehicles or pedestrians, however, establishing the existence of racial profiling and quantifying its impact is extremely difficult because of the complexities inherent in determining the extent to which the disparities reflect racial bias or legitimate factors. Nevertheless, in many studies researchers conclude that race-neutral factors cannot wholly account for the disparities. Thus, for example, researchers have concluded that legitimate race-neutral reasons do not explain all of the stark racial disparities evident in New York City police "stop and frisk" decisions.

Disproportionate Incarceration Rates

Racial disparities evident in drug arrests grow larger as cases wind their way through the criminal justice system. Thus, blacks constitute 43 percent and whites 55 percent of persons convicted of drug felonies in state courts, and then the disproportion increases slightly among people sent to prison because of drug convictions (with blacks accounting for 53.5 percent and whites 33.3 percent, as discussed above). Prosecutorial discretion may play a role in the increased disparity between arrests and prison admissions for drug offenses, as prosecutors have essentially unchecked authority to choose what charges to bring and what pleas to accept. Blacks arrested on drug charges may also have higher prison admission rates because they are less likely to be able to afford private attorneys and must rely on public defenders overwhelmed with high case loads, court-appointed attorneys who may lack the capacity and/or inclination to vigorously pursue a defense, or private attorneys who have little incentive to put anything beyond the least amount of time into a case because they have contracted at a fixed price to take on public defense cases. Although defendants represented by publicly financed counsel have the same conviction rates as those represented by private attorneys, those with publicly financed counsel are more likely to be sentenced to incarceration.

Drug law enforcement has deepened the racial disadvantages confronted by low-income African Americans even as it perpetuates the erroneous belief that most drug offenders are black.

Another factor to consider as an explanation for higher prison admission rates is the existence of a prior criminal record, which increases the likelihood of a prison sentence upon a subsequent conviction. Most states have enhanced penalties for second or subsequent drug offenses. Since blacks are more likely to be arrested and hence more likely to have prior convictions, they are more likely to receive prison sentences for subsequent offenses. . . .

Racial Injustice and Human Rights

In the post–civil rights era in the US, deep racial inequities remain in the criminal justice system. We do not know whether or to what extent conscious racism—that is, overt hostility to blacks—affects the actions of individual police, prosecutors, judges, politicians, or other participants in drug law enforcement. What we can identify are institutional structures and practices that appear to be color-blind but have the effect of perpetuating advantages for whites and disadvantages for blacks. The "war on drugs" is a paradigmatic example. Laws that appear racially neutral are actually embedded in particular racial dynamics adverse to African Americans, and their enforcement perpetuates those dynamics. As Prof. David Cole has observed, inequalities in the criminal justice system "do not stem from explicit and intentional race or class discrimination, but they are problems of inequality nonetheless." The problem is not explicit and intentional considerations of race, but racial "disparities built into the very structure and doctrine of our criminal justice system. . . ."

Drug law enforcement has deepened the racial disadvantages confronted by low-income African Americans even as it perpetuates the erroneous belief that most drug offenders are black. Research shows that "at a time when civil rights and welfare policies aimed at improving opportunities and living standards for black Americans, drug and crime policies worsened them . . . [They] have operated in the same ways as slavery and 'Jim Crow' legalized discrimination did in earlier periods to de-stabilize black communities and disadvantage black Americans, especially black American men." The Leadership Conference on Civil Rights concluded in a study of civil rights and the criminal justice system, "Our criminal laws, while facially neutral, are enforced in a manner that is massively and pervasively biased. The injustices of the criminal justice system threaten to render irrelevant fifty years of hard-fought civil rights progress."

Harsher Sentences for Crack over Powder Cocaine Are Unfair

Richard Durbin

U.S. senator Richard Durbin is a Democrat from Illinois. Elected in 1996, he became the Democratic whip—the second-ranking member of the party in the Senate—in 2005.

I rise to speak about the Fair Sentencing Act of 2009, which I am introducing today [October 15, 2009].

This narrowly tailored bill would eliminate the sentencing disparity that exists in the United States between crack cocaine and powder cocaine. At the same time, it would increase penalties for the worst offenders for crimes involving these substances. It accomplishes two very important goals: One goal is to restore fairness to drug sentencing and, second, to focus our limited Federal resources on the most effective way to end violent drug trafficking.

A Mistaken Act

I have cast thousands of votes as a Member of the House of Representatives and the Senate. Most of those votes are kind of lost in the shadows of history. Some were historic, relative to going to war and impeachment issues, and you never forget those.

But there was one vote I cast more than 20 years ago which I regret. It was a vote that was cast by many of us in the House of Representatives, when we were first informed about the appearance of a new narcotic on the streets. It was called crack cocaine. It was so cheap it was going to be plenti-

Richard Durbin, "Introducing S. 1789," *Congressional Record*, October 15, 2009, pp. S10490–S10492.

ful, and it was so insidious—or at least we were told that 20 years ago—we were advised to take notice and do something dramatic and we did.

More than 20 years ago, I joined many Members of Congress from both political parties in voting for the Anti-Drug Abuse Act of 1986. It established the Federal cocaine sentencing framework that is still in place today.

Under this law, it takes 100 times more powder cocaine than crack cocaine to trigger the same 5-to-10-year mandatory minimum sentence. This is known as the 100-to-1 crack/powder sentencing disparity. But that phrase doesn't tell the story. Here is the story. Simply possessing 5 grams of crack, which is the equivalent of holding five packets of sugar or Equal or one of the sugar substitutes, simply possessing that small amount of crack cocaine under the current sentencing framework carries the same sentence as selling—not possessing but selling—500 grams of powder cocaine—the equivalent of 500 packets of sugar. Why? Well, because we believed we were dealing with a different class of narcotics; something that was much more dangerous and should be treated much more harshly.

Make no mistake, cocaine—whether in crack or powder form—has a devastating impact on families and on our society and we need to have tough legislation when it comes to narcotics. But in addition to being tough, our drug laws have to be fair.

An Unjustified Disparity

Right now, our cocaine laws are based on a distinction between crack and powder cocaine which cannot be justified. Our laws don't focus on the most dangerous offenders. Incarcerating for 5 to 10 years people who are possessing five sugar packets' worth of crack cocaine for the same period of time as those who are selling 500 sugar-size packets of powder cocaine is indefensible.

The Fair Sentencing Act, which I am introducing today, would completely eliminate this crack/powder disparity. It establishes the same sentences for crack and powder—a 1-to-1 sentencing ratio.

Those of us who supported the law establishing this disparity had good intentions. We followed the lead and advice of people in law enforcement. We wanted to address this crack epidemic that was spreading fear and ravaging communities. But we have learned a great deal in the last 20 years. We now know the assumptions that led us to create this disparity were wrong.

Our cocaine laws are based on a distinction between crack and powder cocaine which cannot be justified.

Myths About Crack

Vice President Joe Biden, one of the authors of the legislation creating this disparity in sentencing, has said: "Each of the myths upon which we based the disparity has since been dispelled or altered."

Earlier this year [2009], I held a hearing in the Senate Judiciary Committee on this disparity in sentencing and we learned the following: Crack is not more addictive than powder cocaine, and crack cocaine offenses do not involve significantly more violence than powder cocaine offenses. Those were the two things that led us to this gross disparity in sentencing between powder cocaine and crack cocaine. We were told it is different; it is more addictive. It is not. We were also told it was going to create conduct which was much more violent than those who were selling powder cocaine and their activities. It did not.

We have also learned that more than 2.3 million people are imprisoned in America today. That is the most prisoners and the highest per capita rate of prisoners of any country in the world, and it is largely due to the incarceration of nonviolent drug offenders in America. African Americans are incarcerated at nearly six times the rate of White Americans. These are issues of fundamental human rights and justice our country must face.

An Unfair Disparity

It is important to note that the crack/powder disparity disproportionately affects African Americans. While African Americans constitute less than 30 percent of crack users, they make up 82 percent of those convicted of Federal crack offenses.

At a hearing I held, we heard compelling testimony from Judge Reggie B. Walton, who was Associate Director of the Office of Drug Control Policy under President George H.W. Bush and was appointed by President George W. Bush to the Federal bench. Judge Walton is an African American, and he testified about "the agony of having to enforce a law that one believes is fundamentally unfair and disproportionately impacts individuals who look like me."

We also heard about the negative impact the crack/powder disparity has on the criminal justice system. Judge Walton further testified about "jurors who would tell me that they refused to convict, that even though they thought the evidence was overwhelming, they were not prepared to put another young black man in prison knowing the sentencing disparity that existed between crack and powder cocaine."

Asa Hutchinson, who was head of the Drug Enforcement Administration under President George W. Bush, testified: "Under the current disparity, the credibility of our entire drug enforcement system is weakened."

The crack disparity also diverts resources away from the prosecution of large-scale drug traffickers. In fact, more than 60 percent of defendants convicted of Federal crack crimes are street-level dealers or mules.

During these difficult economic times, it is also important to note that the crack/powder disparity has placed an enormous burden on taxpayers and the prison system. Based on the Bureau of Prison's estimates of the annual costs of incarceration and the U.S. Sentencing Commission's projections of the number of prison beds reduced per year, we know that eliminating this disparity could save more than $510 million in prison beds over 15 years.

Support for the Bill

There is widespread and growing agreement that the Federal cocaine and sentencing policy in the United States today is unjustified and unjust.

At the hearing I held on the crack/powder disparity, Lanny Breuer, the Assistant Attorney General of the Criminal Division, announced that the Justice Department and [the Barack Obama] administration support completely eliminating the crack/powder disparity and establishing a 1-to-1 ratio, which is included in my bill.

In June [2009], Attorney General Eric Holder testified before the Senate Judiciary Committee. I asked him about this issue and here is what he said.

> When one looks at the racial implications of the crack-powder disparity, it has bred disrespect for our criminal justice system. It has made the job of those of us in law enforcement more difficult.... [I]t is time to do away with that disparity.

Here on Capitol Hill, Democrats and Republicans alike have advocated fixing the disparity for years.

The following 10 Senators are original cosponsors of the Fair Sentencing Act: Senator Patrick Leahy, the Chairman of the Judiciary Committee, who for years has advocated for drug sentencing reform; Senator Arlen Specter, the Chair of the Judiciary Committee's Crime and Drugs Subcommittee;

Five other members of the Senate Judiciary Committee—Senators Russ Feingold, Ben Cardin, Sheldon Whitehouse, Ted Kaufman, and Al Franken; and Senators John Kerry, Chris Dodd, and Carl Levin.

I would also like to recognize at this point, though he is not a cosponsor of the bill, Senator Jeff Sessions, the ranking member of the Judiciary Committee. He has been a leader in calling for reform of crack/powder sentencing policy.

The Senator from Alabama is a former U.S. attorney, not known to be soft on crime in any way, shape, or form, but he was one of the first to speak out about the injustice of the crack/powder disparity. I continue my dialog with Senator Sessions in the hope that he and I can come to a common place with regard to this important issue.

There is a bipartisan consensus about the need to fix the crack-powder disparity. I have been in discussions with Chairman Leahy and Ranking Member Sessions, as well as Republican Senators Lindsey Graham, Orrin Hatch, and Tom Coburn, and I am confident that the Judiciary Committee can come together to find a bipartisan solution to this problem.

A broad coalition of legal, law enforcement, civil rights, and religious leaders and groups from across the political spectrum supports eliminating the crack-powder disparity, including, for example: Los Angeles Police Chief Bill Bratton, Miami Police Chief John Timoney, The American Bar Association, The Leadership Conference on Civil Rights, The National Black Police Association, and The United Methodist Church.

The Fair Sentencing Act

The bipartisan United States Sentencing Commission has been urging Congress to act for 15 years. They have argued that fixing the crack-powder disparity "would better reduce the [sentencing] gap [between African Americans and whites] than any other single policy change, and it would dramatically improve the fairness of the federal sentencing system." The Sentencing Commission has repeatedly recommended that Congress take two important steps: No. 1, reduce the sentencing disparity by increasing the quantities of crack cocaine that trigger mandatory minimum sentences; and No. 2, eliminate the mandatory minimum penalty for simple possession of crack cocaine. This is the only mandatory minimum sentence for simple possession of a drug by a first time offender.

The bill that I have introduced does both those things.

In order to ensure that limited Federal resources are directed toward the largest drug traffickers and the most violent offenders, not just those guilty of simple possession and a first offense, the Fair Sentencing Act provides for increased penalties for drug offenses involving vulnerable victims, violence and other aggravating factors.

For example, an individual being prosecuted for possessing either crack or powder cocaine will face more jail time if he: uses or threatens to use violence; uses or possesses a dangerous weapon; is a manager, leader or organizer of drug trafficking activities; or distributes drugs to a pregnant woman or minor.

The bill would also increase the financial penalties for drug trafficking. This sentencing structure will shift Federal resources towards violent traffickers and away from nonviolent drug users who are best dealt with at the State level.

In the final analysis, this legislation is about fixing an unjust law that has taken a great human toll.

A Casualty of Unjust Law

In the final analysis, this legislation is about fixing an unjust law that has taken a great human toll. At the hearing I held in the Judiciary Committee, we heard testimony from Cedric Parker, who is from Alton in my home State of Illinois. In 2000, Mr. Parker's sister, Eugenia Jennings, was sentenced to

22 years in prison for selling 14 grams of crack cocaine. Mr. Parker told us that Eugenia was physically and sexually abused from a young age. She was addicted to crack by the time she was 15.

Eugenia has three children, Radley, Radeisha, and Cardez. They are now 11, 14, and 15. These children were 2, 5, and 6 when their mother went to prison for selling the equivalent of 6 sugar cubes of crack. They have seen their mother once in the last 9 years. They will be 21, 24, and 25 when she is released in 2019.

At Eugenia's sentencing, Judge Patrick Murphy said this:

> Mrs. Jennings, nobody has ever been there for you when you needed it. When you were a child and you were being abused, the Government wasn't there. But when you had a little bit of crack, the government was there. And it is an awful thing, an awful thing to separate a mother from her children. That's what the Government has done for Eugenia Jennings.

It is time to right this wrong. We have talked about the need to address the crack-powder disparity for long enough. Now, it's time to act. I urge my colleagues to join me in supporting the Fair Sentencing Act of 2009. [Editor's note: The Fair Sentencing Act became Public Law 111-220 in August 2010.]

The United States Should Continue the War on Illegal Drugs

John P. Walters

John P. Walters is executive vice president of the Hudson Institute and was director of the Office of National Drug Control Policy from 2001 to 2009 under President George W. Bush.

Justified alarm over drug-related Mexican border violence has led to the predictable spate of drug legalization proposals. The most prominent was a call by three former Latin American presidents—from Brazil, Colombia and Mexico—to end what they claimed was the drug war. While there are many "end the drug war" plans, all of them, as even their advocates admit, result in more drug use and addiction. Their response? We should emasculate prevention and law enforcement and just spend more on treatment.

What would America look like with twice or three times as many drug users and addicts? To answer, consider what America was like in the recent past, during the frightening epidemic of methamphetamine, so similar to the crack outbreak of the 1980s. Each was a nightmare, fueled by ready drug availability.

Americans can't forget the meth epidemic hitting the heartland earlier this decade. In 2004, 1.4 million people said they had used methamphetamine in the past year, according to the National Survey on Drug Use and Health. The powerful, long-lasting stimulant began growing rapidly as the make-it-yourself drug, using a precursor in over-the-counter cold medicine. It later was produced in large quantities by Mexican traffickers and smuggled into the U.S. Drugs weren't just an urban problem anymore.

Addiction, violence and drug poison hammered middle America. The addiction epidemic shattered families and created a staggering toll of family violence. Effective laws got the addicted into treatment through the courts, and thereby saved lives. In parallel, we deployed targeted prevention measures and, importantly, used law enforcement and regulation to cut meth production dramatically. As a result, use (as measured by workplace drug testing and youth surveys) and supply (as measured by the Drug Enforcement Administration [DEA]) dropped sharply: by 60% or more between 2002 and 2008.

Cocaine and crack present a comparable case study. Urban policy experts on the left and right—who agree about little else—have a united view of what cocaine and crack did to our urban poor. Pushing back against crack made urban life better for all Americans.

The violence of traffickers . . . is dwarfed by the millions harmed by another violence, that done daily by those in our own communities under the influence of drugs.

The violence essential to drug trafficking is meant to be shocking—from the marijuana traffickers who brutally murdered DEA special agent Enrique "Kiki" Camarena in Mexico in 1985 to the viciousness of rolling heads across a dance floor—calculated to frighten decent citizens and government authorities into silence.

The violence of traffickers, which has harmed tens of thousands, is dwarfed by the millions harmed by another violence, that done daily by those in our own communities under the influence of drugs. Roughly 80% of child abuse and neglect cases are tied to the use and abuse of drugs. It is not that drug abuse causes all crime and violence, it just makes it much worse by impairing judgment, weakening impulse control and at some levels of pathology, with some drugs, causing paranoia and psychosis. Well more than 50% of those arrested today for violent and property crimes test positive for illegal drug use when arrested. Legalized access to drugs would increase drug-related suffering dramatically.

The origins of federal drug laws were a response to disastrous drug and violence epidemics when virtually every family had access to opiate- and cocaine-based remedies around the end of the 19th century. Drugs were available without penalty. Addiction was rampant, with an estimated 250,000 opiate addicts in the U.S. population of 76 million.

Although cynics on the left and right assert the drug problem is as big or bigger than ever, it is simply not true.

Or if you really think that prohibition causes the problem, remember that ancient China was brought to its knees by easy access to opium. Today, even highly traditional and regulated societies like Thailand, Malaysia, Iran and Afghanistan are suffering terrible addiction problems—because heroin is addictive and easily accessible. Making highly addictive drugs easier to get and use is what makes this harm greater.

Although cynics on the left and right assert the drug problem is as big or bigger than ever, it is simply not true. Illegal drug use is still a problem, but by any fair assessment it is a smaller problem. Half as many teens are using drugs than 30 years ago and a quarter fewer than seven years ago, according to the Monitoring the Future [survey], an ongoing study conducted by the University of Michigan under grants from the National Institute on Drug Abuse. Cocaine and meth use are less than half what they were at their peak. Even drug offenders are a smaller percentage of the prison population than they were 15 or even seven years ago.

What are the indelible lessons? In the process of making the drug problem much smaller, we learned the importance of education—not principally teaching the young about the health dangers of specific drugs, but teaching young and old about the disease of addiction. We know that the disease begins with the use of addictive drugs and that those drugs change the brain—they create craving, impair judgment and lead to withdrawal or a feeling of illness in absence of the drug. Science has helped us see that we need to help those who are addicted particularly when they do not want our help—every family of an addict or alcoholic knows that denial is a terrible part of this disease.

When I became the drug policy director in 2001, we faced an inherent weakness in prevention programs for youth. Teens told us they had been taught the dangers of drugs, but if their boyfriend or girlfriend used they did not want to be judgmental or estranged, so they were likely to join in. We put treatment specialists together with some of the best creative minds in advertising to fashion prevention messages directly presenting drug abuse as a sickness that places an obligation on friends to help stop it. We enlisted the idealism and caring of the young to reverse the force of peer pressure. The ads were an important contributor to our progress that needs to continue and grow. With this knowledge of addiction, how do we choose to make more victims?

We have learned to apply public health tools that have been proven effective against other diseases. We have learned that addiction is a treatable disease. We are increasing the pathways to treatment—through routine health care, the workplace, places of worship and schools. Drug courts leading to referral for treatment by the criminal justice system are now the major pathway through which the dependent are getting the help they need. Do we want to end all this by taking the courts out of the equation? Supervised, court-sanctioned treatment works best. Legalization robs us of this tool.

We have also learned how to join law enforcement and national security resources to break down trafficking groups and narcoterrorists. One of the greatest international policy success stories of the last decade has been the transformation of Colombia from a state dominated by narcoterrorism, violence and corruption to a thriving liberal democracy.

Between 2001 and 2007, the U.S. government's estimate of the maximum potential production of cocaine in Colombia dropped 24%. There is no certain method of translating that into drug profits, but even conservative estimates show that a 24% reduction equaled hundreds of millions of dollars in lost revenue. There is now evidence that the combined effect of reduced production and increased seizures dropped the available Colombian cocaine supply to the U.S. from 2001 to 2007.

Just as ending Prohibition did not destroy organized crime in the U.S., legalizing drugs will not break the terrorist criminal groups in Mexico.

Colombia is the genuine backdrop for understanding the threat in Mexico today. The criminal gangs in Mexico go back decades. Many are drawn from generations in the same extended families. They have become wealthier and better armed, but the border areas they seek to control are an old battleground. The corruption they use to protect themselves has deep roots. They have become more dangerous as they have lost profits from the cocaine and meth trade over the last two years. Those who think legalizing drugs will stop the violence by cutting off the money to these groups seem unaware that they not only smuggle drugs and people across the border for profit, but that they also kidnap, hijack, manage large auto-theft operations and have extensive protection rackets.

Moreover, some of us remember that [John F. Kennedy administration attorney general] Bobby Kennedy was leading organized-crime strike forces against extremely dangerous mafia families, decades after the end of Prohibition. Just as ending Prohibition did not destroy organized crime in the U.S., legalizing drugs will not break the terrorist criminal groups in Mexico. In fact, the real pattern of violence from the mafia families in the U.S. to the cartels in Colombia suggests it is when they are threatened and destabilized that violence skyrockets. It is the violence focused on the threat of violent takeover by rival criminal groups that is an unfortunate but perhaps necessary first step in restoring the rule of law.

Legalizing drugs is the worst thing we could do for President Felipe Calderón and our Mexican allies. It would weaken the moral authority of his fight and the Mexicans would immediately realize that we have no intention of reducing consumption. Who do we think would take the profits from a legal drug trade? U.S. suppliers would certainly spring up, but that wouldn't preclude Mexican supplies as well—or Mexican production for consumption in other countries. The Mexicans know that they too have a dangerous use and addiction problem. They have already learned that it is wrong and dangerous to make abuse and addiction worse.

We can make progress faster when more of us learn that drug use and addiction cannot be an expression of individual liberty in a free society. Drug abuse is, by nature and the laws of organic chemistry that govern this disease, incompatible with freedom and civil society. Drug abuse makes human life solitary, poor, nasty, brutish and short (a special version of [philosopher Thomas] Hobbes's hell in our own families). In the deepest sense, this is why failure is not an option.

U.S. Drug Law Enforcement Is Not Racially Unjust

Heather Mac Donald

Heather Mac Donald is John M. Olin Fellow at the Manhattan Institute for Policy Research and a contributing editor to City Journal.

The race industry and its elite enablers take it as self-evident that high black incarceration rates result from discrimination. At a presidential primary debate this Martin Luther King Day [2008], for instance, Senator Barack Obama charged that blacks and whites "are arrested at very different rates, are convicted at very different rates, [and] receive very different sentences . . . for the same crime." Not to be outdone, Senator Hillary Clinton promptly denounced the "disgrace of a criminal-justice system that incarcerates so many more African-Americans proportionately than whites."

Accusations of Disparate Treatment

If a listener didn't know anything about crime, such charges of disparate treatment might seem plausible. After all, in 2006, blacks were 37.5 percent of all state and federal prisoners, though they're under 13 percent of the national population. About one in 33 black men was in prison in 2006, compared with one in 205 white men and one in 79 Hispanic men. Eleven percent of all black males between the ages of 20 and 34 are in prison or jail. The dramatic rise in the prison and jail population over the last three decades—to 2.3 million people at the end of 2007—has only amplified the racial accusations against the criminal-justice system.

The favorite culprits for high black prison rates include a biased legal system, draconian drug enforcement, and even prison itself. None of these explanations stands up to scrutiny. The black incarceration rate is overwhelmingly a function of black crime. Insisting otherwise only worsens black alienation and further defers a real solution to the black crime problem.

Racial activists usually remain assiduously silent about that problem. But in 2005, the black homicide rate was over seven times higher than that of whites and Hispanics combined, according to the federal Bureau of Justice Statistics. From 1976 to 2005, blacks committed over 52 percent of all murders in America. In 2006, the black arrest rate for most crimes was two to nearly three times blacks' representation in the population. Blacks constituted 39.3 percent of all violent-crime arrests, including 56.3 percent of all robbery and 34.5 percent of all aggravated-assault arrests, and 29.4 percent of all property-crime arrests.

The advocates acknowledge such crime data only indirectly: by charging bias on the part of the system's decision makers. As Obama suggested in the Martin Luther King debate, police, prosecutors, and judges treat blacks and whites differently "for the same crime."

The Charge of Racial Bias

Let's start with the idea that cops over-arrest blacks and ignore white criminals. In fact, the race of criminals reported by crime victims matches arrest data. As long ago as 1978, a study of robbery and aggravated assault in eight cities found parity between the race of assailants in victim identifications and in arrests—a finding replicated many times since, across a range of crimes. No one has ever come up with a plausible argument as to why crime victims would be biased in their reports.

Moving up the enforcement chain, the campaign against the criminal-justice system next claims that prosecutors overcharge and judges oversentence blacks. Obama describes this alleged postarrest treatment as "Scooter Libby [a convicted government official whose penalties were reduced] justice for some and Jena justice for others." Jena, Louisiana, of course, was where a D.A. [district attorney] initially lodged attempted second-degree murder charges against black students who, in December 2006, slammed a white student's head against a concrete beam, knocking him unconscious, and then stomped and kicked him in the head while he was down. As [writer] Charlotte Allen has brilliantly chronicled in *The Weekly Standard*, a local civil rights activist crafted a narrative linking the attack to an unrelated incident months earlier, in which three white students hung two nooses from a schoolyard tree—a display that may or may not have been intended as a racial provocation. This entrepreneur then embellished the tale with other alleged instances of redneck racism—above all, the initial attempted-murder charges. An enthusiastic national press responded to the bait exactly as intended, transforming the "Jena Six" into victims rather than perpetrators. In the seven months of ensuing headlines and protests, Jena became a symbol of systemic racial unfairness in America's court system. If blacks were disproportionately in prison, the refrain went, it was because they faced biased prosecutors—like the one in Jena—as well as biased juries and judges.

Backing up this bias claim has been the holy grail of criminology for decades—and the prize remains as elusive as ever. In 1997, criminologists Robert Sampson and Janet Lauritsen reviewed the massive literature on charging and sentencing. They concluded that "large racial differences in criminal offending," not racism, explained why more blacks were in prison proportionately than whites and for longer terms. A 1987 analysis of Georgia felony convictions, for example, found that blacks frequently received disproportionately lenient punishment. A 1990 study of 11,000 California cases found that slight racial disparities in sentence length resulted from blacks' prior records and other legally relevant variables. A 1994 Justice Department survey of felony cases from the country's 75 largest urban areas discovered that blacks actually had a lower chance of prosecution following a felony than whites did and that they were less likely to be found guilty at trial. Following conviction, blacks were more likely to receive prison sentences, however—an outcome that reflected the gravity of their offenses as well as their criminal records. . . .

The media love to target the federal crack penalties because crack defendants are likely to be black.

Federal Crack Penalties

Unfair drug policies are an equally popular explanation for black incarceration rates. Legions of pundits, activists, and academics charge that the war on drugs is a war on minorities—a de facto war at best, an intentional one at worst.

Playing a starring role in this conceit are federal crack penalties, the source of the greatest amount of misinformation in the race and incarceration debate. Crack is a smokeable and highly addictive cocaine concentrate, created by cooking powder cocaine until it hardens into pellets called "rocks." Crack produces a faster—and more potent—high than powder cocaine, and it's easier to use, since smoking avoids the unpleasantness of needles and is more efficient than snorting. Under the 1986 federal Anti-Drug Abuse Act, getting caught with five grams of crack carries a mandatory minimum five-year sentence in federal court; to trigger the same five-year minimum, powder-cocaine traffickers would have to get caught with 500 grams. On average, federal crack sentences are three to six times longer than powder sentences for equivalent amounts.

The media love to target the federal crack penalties because crack defendants are likely to be black. In 2006, 81 percent of federal crack defendants were black, while only 27 percent of federal powder-cocaine defendants were. Since federal crack rules are more severe than those for powder, and crack offenders are disproportionately black, those rules must explain why so many blacks are in prison, the conventional wisdom holds.

But consider the actual number of crack sellers sentenced in federal court each year. In 2006, 5,619 were tried federally, 4,495 of them black. From 1996 to 2000, the federal courts sentenced more powder traffickers (23,743) than crack traffickers (23,121). It's going to take a lot more than 5,000 or so crack defendants a year to account for the 562,000 black prisoners in state and federal facilities at the end of 2006—or the 858,000 black prisoners in custody overall, if one includes the population of county and city jails. Nor do crack/powder disparities at the state level explain black incarceration rates: only 13 states distinguish between crack and powder sentences, and they employ much smaller sentence differentials.

The press almost never mentions the federal methamphetamine-trafficking penalties, which are identical to those for crack: five grams of meth net you a mandatory minimum five-year sentence. In 2006, the 5,391 sentenced federal meth defendants (nearly as many as the crack defendants) were 54 percent white, 39 percent Hispanic, and 2 percent black. But no one calls the federal meth laws anti-Hispanic or anti-white.

A Revisionist Narrative

Nevertheless, the federal crack penalties dominate discussions on race and incarceration because they seem to provide a concrete example of egregious racial disparity. This leads to a commonly expressed syllogism: crack penalties have a disparate impact on blacks; disparate impact is racist; therefore, crack penalties are racist. This syllogism has been particularly prominent recently, thanks to the U.S. Sentencing Commission's 2007 decision to lighten federal crack penalties retroactively in the name of racial equity.

The press has covered this development voraciously, serving up a massive dose of crack revisionism aimed at proving the racist origins of the war on crack. Crack was never a big deal, the revisionist story line goes. But when Boston Celtics draft pick Len Bias died of a crack overdose in 1986, the media went into overdrive covering the crack phenomenon. "Images—or perhaps anecdotes—about the evils of crack, and the street crime it was presumed to stoke" circulated, as the *New York Times* archly put it in a December 2007 article. A "moral panic" (Michael Tonry's term) ensued about an imaginary threat from a powerless minority group. Whites feared that addicted blacks would invade their neighborhoods. Sensational stories about "crack babies" surfaced. All this hysteria resulted in the unnecessary federal crack penalties.

Since the 1980s, the revisionist narrative continues, experts have determined that powder and crack show more pharmacological "similarities than differences," in the *Times*'s words, and that crack is no more damaging to fetuses than alcohol. The belief that crack was an inner-city scourge was thus a racist illusion, and the sentencing structure to quell it a racist assault. Or, as U.S. District Judge Clyde Cahill put it, in what one hopes is not a representative sample of the federal judicial temperament: "Legislators' unconscious racial aversion towards blacks, sparked by unsubstantiated reports of the effects of crack, reactionary media prodding, and an agitated constituency, motivated the legislators . . . to produce a dual system of punishment."

The biggest problem with the revisionist narrative is its unreality.

Leave aside the irony of the press's now declaring smugly that the press exaggerated the ravages of crack. (The same *New York Times* that now sneers at "images—or perhaps anecdotes—about the evils of crack" ran searing photos of crack addicts in 1993 that included a woman kneeling before a crack dealer, unzipping his fly, a baby clinging to her back; such degraded prostitutes, known as "strawberries," were pervasive casualties of the epidemic.) The biggest problem with the revisionist narrative is its unreality. The assertion that concern about crack resulted from "unconscious racial aversion towards blacks" ignores a key fact: black leaders were the first to sound the alarm about the drug, as Harvard law professor Randall Kennedy documents in *Race, Crime, and the Law*. Harlem congressman Charles Rangel initiated the federal response to the epidemic, warning the House of Representatives in March 1986 that crack had made cocaine "frightening[ly]" accessible to youth. A few months later, Brooklyn congressman Major Owens explicitly rejected what is now received wisdom about media hype. "None of the press accounts really have exaggerated what is actually going on," Owens said; the crack epidemic was "as bad as any articles have stated." Queens congressman Alton Waldon then called on his colleagues to act: "For those of us who are black this self-inflicted pain is the worst oppression we have known since slavery. . . . Let us . . . pledge to crack down on crack." The bill that eventually passed, containing the crack/powder distinction, won majority support among black congressmen, none of whom, as Kennedy points out, objected to it as racist.

Protecting the Black Community

These politicians were reacting to a devastating outbreak of inner-city violence and addiction unleashed by the new form of cocaine. Because crack came in small, easily digestible amounts, it democratized what had been a rarefied drug, making an intense high available to people with very little money. The crack market differed radically from the discreet phone transactions and private deliveries that characterized powder-cocaine distribution: volatile young dealers sold crack on street corners, using guns to establish their turf. Crack, homicides, and assaults went hand in hand; certain areas of New York became "like a war zone," retired DEA [Drug Enforcement Administration] special agent Robert Stutman told PBS's *Frontline* in 2000. The large national spike in violence in the mid-1980s was largely due to the crack trade, and its victims were overwhelmingly black inner-city residents.

What led to the crack-sentencing scheme wasn't racism but legal logic.

Though the elites are furiously rewriting crack history, many people who lived through it are not. In April 2007, Los Angeles prosecutor Robert Grace won the conviction of a crack dealer who had raped and strangled to death ten strawberries between 1987 and 1998. The "crack epidemic was one of the worst things that happened to the black and brown community," Grace asserts. Matthew Kennedy managed an infamous public housing project in Watts [a Los Angeles neighborhood] during the crack epidemic. "Some of us remember how bad it was," he says. When children avoid school for fear of getting shot by drug gangs, "you've just lost that generation." Lawrence Tolliver has witnessed his share of shootings outside his South Central [Los Angeles] barbershop. "Sometimes it was so bad you had to scout the horizon like a gazelle at a watering hole in Africa," he recalls.

It takes shameless sleight of hand to turn an effort to protect blacks into a conspiracy against them. If Congress had ignored black legislators' calls to increase cocaine-trafficking penalties, the outcry among the groups now crying racism would have been deafening. Yes, a legislative bidding war drove federal crack penalties ultimately to an arbitrary and excessive point; the reduction of those penalties is appropriate. But what led to the crack-sentencing scheme wasn't racism but legal logic. Prosecutors rely on heavy statutory penalties to induce defendants to spill the beans on their criminal colleagues.

"An amazing public spirit is engendered when you tell someone he is facing 150 years to life but has the possibility of getting out after eight if he tells you who committed a string of homicides," says Walter Arsenault, who headed the Manhattan district attorney's homicide-investigation unit in the 1980s and 1990s.

A Rational Distinction

Race activists endlessly promote the claim that the draconian federal crack laws are sweeping up mere sad sacks with a little extra crack to spare. But anyone who fits that description is exempt from the federal sentencing scheme. Traffickers with only a modest criminal history who didn't injure others or have a gun when arrested can escape the mandatory federal sentences if they don't lie to the government about their offense (there is no requirement to rat out others). In 2006, only 15.4 percent of crack-cocaine defendants qualified for this safety-valve provision, compared with 48.4 percent of powder-cocaine offenders; in 2000, even fewer crack defendants qualified—12.6 percent. Crack sellers seldom merit the escape clause because their criminal histories tend to be much more severe than powder sellers' and because they're more likely to have or use weapons. The congressional distinction between crack and powder sellers, it turns out, had a firm grounding.

Equally misleading is the criticism that few crack "kingpins" can be found in federal prison. This is not surprising, because "kingpins" in the traditional sense—heads of major drug-importing rings—don't exist in the crack world. Crack is not imported but cooked up locally. Its supply and distribution scheme is more horizontal than vertical, unlike that of powder cocaine and heroin. Federal crack enforcement wasn't about stopping the flow of illegal drugs into the country; it was about stopping urban violence. And that violence was coming from street dealers.

Racial Disparities in Prison

Critics follow up their charges about crack with several empirical claims about drugs and imprisonment. None is true. The first is that drug enforcement has been the most important cause of the overall rising incarceration rate since the 1980s. Yet even during the most rapid period of population growth in prisons—from 1980 to 1990—36 percent of the growth in state prisons (where 88 percent of the nation's prisoners are housed) came from violent crimes, compared with 33 percent from drug crimes. Since then, drug offenders have played an even smaller role in state prison expansion.

So much for the claim that blacks are disproportionately imprisoned because of the war on drugs.

From 1990 to 2000, violent offenders accounted for 53 percent of the census increase—and all of the increase from 1999 to 2004.

Next, critics blame drug enforcement for rising racial disparities in prison. Again, the facts say otherwise. In 2006, blacks were 37.5 percent of the 1,274,600 state prisoners. If you remove drug prisoners from that population, the percentage of black prisoners drops to 37 percent—half of a percentage point, hardly a significant difference. (No criminologist, to the best of my knowledge, has ever performed this exercise.)

The rise of drug cases in the criminal-justice system has been dramatic, it's important to acknowledge. In 1979, drug offenders were 6.4 percent of the state prison population; in 2004, they were 20 percent. Even so, violent and property offenders continue to dominate the ranks: in 2004, 52 percent of state prisoners were serving time for violence and 21 percent for property crimes, for a combined total over three and a half times that of state drug offenders. In federal prisons, drug offenders went from 25 percent of all federal inmates in 1980 to 47.6 percent of all federal inmates in 2006. Drug-war opponents focus almost exclusively on federal, as opposed to state, prisons because the proportion of drug offenders is highest there. But the federal system held just 12.3 percent of the nation's prisoners in 2006.

So much for the claim that blacks are disproportionately imprisoned because of the war on drugs.

Harsher Sentences for Crack over Powder Cocaine Are Justified

Bob Bushman

Bob Bushman is vice president of the National Narcotic Officers' Associations' Coalition (NNOAC), a national organization representing forty state narcotic associations.

Technically, what our NNOAC [National Narcotic Officers' Associations' Coalition] members do is enforce the laws against crime and illegal drugs that legislative bodies, like Congress, put on the books.

In human terms, the people we represent are dedicated law enforcement officers. As we testify here today [May 21, 2009], many police officers, sheriff's deputies, and state and federal agents are working in neighborhoods throughout our country, protecting our communities from predators who profit greatly by selling and distributing poisons to our kids with the knowledge that these poisons will make them addicts, expose them to violence, and in some instances, even kill them. These predators purposely harm not only the user, but the user's family, and the community as well. And, in most instances, our members are the only ones that stand in their way.

The Crack Epidemic

I remember the devastation I saw in the 1980s and 90s as a cop working crack cases in our Twin Cities [Minneapolis and St. Paul, Minnesota]. It was unlike anything I or my partners had ever seen. The highest homicide rates most cities have

Bob Bushman, "Unfairness in Federal Cocaine Sentencing: Is It time to Crack the 100 to 1 Disparity?" Hearing Before the Subcommittee on Crime, Terrorism, and Homeland Security, Committee on the Judiciary, United States House of Representatives, May 21, 2009. Reproduced by permission.

ever experienced occurred during the crack epidemic of the late 80s and early 90s. Our country experienced a painful "wake-up call" and acted decisively to get a handle on the problem. The crack trade was responsible for dramatic increases in violent crime and, consequently, it consumed police resources in many of our most urban areas. The negative impact on public safety was staggering. Drive-by shootings, gang wars and home invasions were common occurrences. Citizens—through their elected representatives and leaders—demanded tough measures to bring the situation under control. The current laws related to sentencing of crack offenders were a direct response to the desperate pleas of the law abiding citizens and their families, who became victims trapped in crime-infested neighborhoods.

Drug problems have existed in our nation for a long time. Most people don't realize that the height of drug addiction in this country occurred just after the Civil War when 1 in 200 Americans were addicted to drugs. During our lifetime, drug use peaked during the late 1970s. Since the height of the crack epidemic, drug use—particularly cocaine use—has declined dramatically. I don't think we hear this enough. If the incidents of AIDS or diabetes decreased as dramatically as drug use has, someone would be getting a Nobel Prize.

We view tough drug sentences as a very effective way of getting predators off the streets.

Yes, we continue to have a significant drug problem in this country. But we have made a huge difference in the past 20 years due, in part, to tough criminal sanctions that both prevent drug use and compel cooperation of individuals to take down drug distribution organizations.

The Crack-Powder Disparity

Let me be clear—we understand the sensitivities around the issue of the 100:1 crack-powder disparity [the ratio of greater consequences for crack-related crimes]. We often work in environments where the law and those who enforce it are not respected, whether it's because of perceived racial bias or some other reason. But we need you, our members of Congress, to understand what we as police officers, sheriff's deputies and drug enforcement agents experience and work with every single day of our careers, and to understand that we are dedicated professionals who work hard to protect our citizens, no matter who they are, where they live, or what they believe.

We are caught in the middle on this issue. Our main concern is public safety—that is what we are hired and trained to do. But it is difficult to protect the citizens, especially those in the drug-infested, high crime areas who need us most, when we cannot rid those neighborhoods of the ones who abuse them the most—drug dealers and gangs. We are criticized by some for not doing enough, and by others for being too aggressive in our prosecution of drug violators.

I can tell you that we view tough drug sentences as a very effective way of getting predators off the streets—we are talking about the dealers and profiteers, *not* the addicts and low-end users. As a matter of fact, many crack dealers do not use crack—they know the dangers of the drug. Mandatory sentences punish the dealer—the people who do the most damage to our communities.

As we talk about the violence associated with the crack cocaine trade, I ask you to remember that it isn't just driven by the dealer's desire to make money or the user's need to get money to purchase crack. Many violent crimes are committed by people who are under the influence of the drug itself, and unable to act rationally. Domestic violence and child abuse are common in crack-riddled neighborhoods. Many police officers and I have spent our own money to purchase food to feed hungry kids whom we found living in crack houses. And, as for those who label drug use or addiction as a "victimless crime," I still haven't found anyone who can explain to me how a crack baby isn't a victim.

We have been asked, repeatedly, over the past few years about our views on legislative proposals to reduce the crack-powder disparity. While we believe that the existing law has been a valuable tool in reducing the impact of crack on communities, we realize that it has also had a negative impact on some people's perception of law enforcement. So, while we agree that it is appropriate for Congress to review the law, we also believe that Congress should consider a solution to narrow the disparity between crack and powder cocaine that includes lowering the threshold quantity for powder cocaine. We do not believe the best approach is to dramatically increase the threshold amount of crack that triggers the minimum penalty.

The Reasons for Harsher Sentences

Why should we continue to maintain tougher sentences for crack than for cocaine powder?

Smoking crack leads to a sudden, short-lived high, causing an intense, immediate desire for more of it. Addiction to crack is quick—and powerful. Just last month [April 2009], the director of the National Institute on Drug Abuse, Dr. Nora Volkow, testified before the Senate Judiciary Committee that "research consistently shows that the form of the drug is not the crucial variable; rather it is the route of administration that accounts for the differences in its behavioral effects."

The violence associated with the crack trade and perpetrated by crack users is more prevalent than that associated with the [powder] cocaine trade; public safety is compromised. We have seen this happen in community after community. Part of it has to do with the turf wars—drug dealers and urban drug gangs fighting for control of an area and the customers it contains. Although much of the violence is dealer-on-dealer, innocent bystanders and, sometimes even entire neighborhoods, are often caught in the cross-fire. These are the citizens that we, as law enforcement officers, are sworn to protect. It's difficult to protect our communities if we can't remove those who are responsible for the crime and violence.

Selling crack is more profitable than selling powder cocaine. If crack cocaine penalties are made equal to that of powder, there will be more incentive to sell crack and make bigger profits. While it is true that crack and powder cocaine have the same physiological effect on the brain, the negative impact on public safety, due to the violence associated with the crack cocaine trade alone, justifies a difference in penalties.

The threat of arrest, prosecution, and imprisonment are important components in deterring drug use, reducing crime and protecting our citizens from falling victim to violent and dangerous, predatory criminals.

The Role of Law Enforcement

We often hear from advocates of drug decriminalization and legalization that "valuable law enforcement resources" are wasted on low-level drug offenders, and that the low thresholds for crack encourage this. I can assure you that state and local law enforcement across the country are not sitting around plotting how to go after users and addicts—we don't have the time or resources to do that. Most of our anti-drug operations in the communities are in direct response to citizens' pleas for help with problems that affect their daily lives and routines—quality of life issues. To the extent that we are dealing with low-level offenders, it is because they are committing other crimes to support their habit or because their actions, while they are under the influence of drugs, threaten the safety of the citizens in our neighborhoods.

As law enforcement professionals, we value the important roles that prevention and education programs play in helping people to avoid immersion into the criminal justice system in the first place. The NNOAC supports, and is involved with, prevention and education programs around the country. But those who do become drug users or addicts need help and, in many cases, the criminal justice system is a gateway to their recovery. We are strong advocates of Drug Court Programs and we believe that they ought to be strengthened and expanded to mitigate the problems caused by drugs in our communities. In fact, our president, Ron Brooks, was just asked to join the board of the National Association of Drug Court Professionals.

We realize we cannot arrest our way out of the drug problem. But the threat of arrest, prosecution, and imprisonment are important components in deterring drug use, reducing crime and protecting our citizens from falling victim to violent and dangerous, predatory criminals.

CHAPTER 3

Should Marijuana Laws Be Relaxed?

Overview: U.S. Federal Policy on Marijuana

Mark Eddy

Mark Eddy is a specialist in crime policy for the Congressional Research Service, a nonpartisan organization providing research to Congress.

The *Cannabis sativa* plant has been used for healing purposes throughout history. According to written records from China and India, the use of marijuana to treat a wide range of ailments goes back more than 2,000 years. Ancient texts from Africa, the Middle East, classical Greece, and the Roman Empire also describe the use of cannabis to treat disease.

For most of American history, growing and using marijuana was legal under both federal law and the laws of the individual states. By the 1840s, marijuana's therapeutic potential began to be recognized by some U.S. physicians. From 1850 to 1941 cannabis was included in the *United States Pharmacopoeia* as a recognized medicinal. By the end of 1936, however, all 48 states had enacted laws to regulate marijuana. Its decline in medicine was hastened by the development of aspirin, morphine, and then other opium-derived drugs, all of which helped to replace marijuana in the treatment of pain and other medical conditions in Western medicine.

All three branches of the federal government play an important role in formulating federal policy on medical marijuana. Significant actions of each branch are highlighted here, beginning with the legislative branch.

The Marihuana Tax Act

Spurred by spectacular accounts of marijuana's harmful effects on its users, by the drug's alleged connection to violent crime,

Mark Eddy, "Medical Marijuana: Review and Analysis of Federal and State Policies," Washington, DC: Congressional Research Service, 2009.

and by a perception that state and local efforts to bring use of the drug under control were not working, Congress enacted the Marihuana Tax Act of 1937. Promoted by Harry Anslinger, Commissioner of the recently established Federal Bureau of Narcotics, the act imposed registration and reporting requirements and a tax on the growers, sellers, and buyers of marijuana. Although the act did not prohibit marijuana outright, its effect was the same. (Because marijuana was not included in the Harrison Narcotics Act in 1914, the Marihuana Tax Act was the federal government's first attempt to regulate marijuana.)

Dr. William C. Woodward, legislative counsel of the American Medical Association (AMA), opposed the measure. In oral testimony before the House Ways and Means Committee, he stated that "there are evidently potentialities in the drug that should not be shut off by adverse legislation. The medical profession and pharmacologists should be left to develop the use of this drug as they see fit." Two months later, in a letter to the Senate Finance Committee, he again argued against the act:

> There is no evidence, however, that the medicinal use of these drugs ["cannabis and its preparations and derivatives"] has caused or is causing cannabis addiction. As remedial agents they are used to an inconsiderable extent, and the obvious purpose and effect of this bill is to impose so many restrictions on their medicinal use as to prevent such use altogether. Since the medicinal use of cannabis has not caused and is not causing addiction, the prevention of the use of the drug for medicinal purposes can accomplish no good end whatsoever. How far it may serve to deprive the public of the benefits of a drug that on further research may prove to be of substantial value, it is impossible to foresee.

Despite the AMA's opposition, the Marihuana Tax Act was approved, causing all medicinal products containing marijuana to be withdrawn from the market and leading to marijuana's removal, in 1941, from *The National Formulary* and the *United States Pharmacopoeia*, in which it had been listed for almost a century.

With increasing use of marijuana and other street drugs during the 1960s, notably by college and high school students, federal drug-control laws came under scrutiny.

The Controlled Substances Act

With increasing use of marijuana and other street drugs during the 1960s, notably by college and high school students, federal drug-control laws came under scrutiny. In July 1969, President [Richard] Nixon asked Congress to enact legislation to combat rising levels of drug use. Hearings were held, different proposals were considered, and House and Senate conferees filed a conference report in October 1970. The report was quickly adopted by voice vote in both chambers and was signed into law as the Comprehensive Drug Abuse Prevention and Control Act of 1970.

Included in the new law was the Controlled Substances Act (CSA), which placed marijuana and its derivatives in Schedule I, the most restrictive of five categories. Schedule I substances have "a high potential for abuse," "no currently accepted medical use in treatment in the United States," and "a lack of accepted safety [standards] for use of the drug . . . under medical supervision." Other drugs used recreationally at the time also became Schedule I substances. These included heroin, LSD, mescaline, peyote, and psilocybin. Drugs of abuse with recognized medical uses—such as opium, cocaine, and amphetamine—were assigned to Schedules II through V, depending on their potential for abuse. Despite its placement in Schedule I, marijuana use increased, as did the number of health-care professionals and their patients who believed in the plant's therapeutic value.

The CSA does not distinguish between the medical and recreational use of marijuana. Under federal statute, simple possession of marijuana for personal use, a misdemeanor, can bring up to one year in federal prison and up to a $100,000 fine for a first offense. Growing marijuana is considered *manufacturing* a controlled substance, a felony. A single plant can bring an individual up to five years in federal prison and up to a $250,000 fine for a first offense.

The CSA is not preempted by state medical marijuana laws, under the federal system of government, nor are state medical marijuana laws preempted by the CSA. States can statutorily create a medical use exception for botanical cannabis and its derivatives under their own, state-level controlled substance laws. At the same time, federal agents can investigate, arrest, and prosecute medical marijuana patients, caregivers, and providers in accordance with the federal Controlled Substances Act, even in those states where medical marijuana programs operate in accordance with state law.

Anti-Medical Marijuana Legislation

In September 1998, the House [of Representatives] debated and passed a resolution declaring that Congress supports the existing federal drug approval process for determining whether any drug, including marijuana, is safe and effective and opposes efforts to circumvent this process by legalizing marijuana, or any other Schedule I drug, for medicinal use without valid scientific evidence and without approval of the Food and Drug Administration (FDA). With the Senate not acting on the resolution and adjournment approaching, this language was incorporated into the FY [fiscal year] 1999 omnibus appropriations act under the heading "Not Legalizing Marijuana for Medicinal Use."

In a separate amendment to the same act, Congress prevented the District of Columbia government from counting ballots of a 1998 voter-approved initiative that would have allowed the medical use of marijuana by persons suffering from serious diseases, including cancer and HIV infection. The amendment was challenged and overturned in District Court, the ballots were counted, and the measure passed 69% to 31%. Nevertheless, despite further court challenges, Congress continues to prohibit implementation of the initiative.

The Hinchey-Rohrabacher Amendment

In the first session of the 108th Congress, in response to federal Drug Enforcement Administration (DEA) raids on medical cannabis users and providers in California and other states that had approved the medical use of marijuana if recommended by a physician, Representatives [Maurice] Hinchey and [Dana] Rohrabacher offered a bipartisan amendment to the FY2004 Commerce, Justice, State appropriations bill. The amendment would have prevented the Justice Department from using appropriated funds to interfere with the implementation of medical cannabis laws in the nine states that had approved such use. The amendment was debated on the floor of the House on July 22, 2003. When brought to a vote on the following day, it was defeated 152 to 273 (61 votes short of passage).

Opponents of the amendment argued, among other things, that its passage would undermine efforts to convince young people that marijuana is a dangerous drug.

The amendment was offered again in the second session of the 108th Congress. It was debated on the House floor on July 7, 2004, during consideration of H.R. 4754, the Commerce, Justice, State appropriations bill for FY2005. This time it would have applied to 10 states, with the recent addition of Vermont to the list of states that had approved the use of medical cannabis. It was again defeated by a similar margin, 148 to 268 (61 votes short of passage).

The amendment was voted on again in the first session of the 109th Congress and was again defeated, 161–264 (52 votes short of passage), on June 15, 2005. During floor debate on H.R. 2862, the FY2006 Science, State, Justice, Commerce appropriations bill, a Member stated in support of the amendment that her now-deceased mother had used marijuana to treat her glaucoma. Opponents of the amendment argued, among other things, that its passage would undermine efforts to convince young people that marijuana is a dangerous drug.

Despite an extensive pre-vote lobbying effort by supporters, the amendment gained only two votes in its favor over the previous year when it was debated and defeated, 163 to 259 (49 votes short of passage), on June 28, 2006. The bill under consideration this time was H.R. 5672, the FY2007 Science, State, Justice, Commerce appropriations bill.

In the first session of the 110th Congress, on July 25, 2007, the amendment was proposed to H.R. 3093, the Commerce, Justice, Science appropriations bill for FY2008. It was debated on the House floor for the fifth time in as many years and was again rejected, 165 to 262 (49 votes short of passage). The amendment's supporters framed it as a states' rights issue:

> A vote "yes" on Hinchey-Rohrabacher is a vote to respect the intent of our Founding Fathers and respect the rights of our people at the State level to make the criminal law under which they and their families will live. It reinforces rules surrounding the patient-doctor relationship, and it is in contrast to emotional posturing and Federal power grabs and bureaucratic arrogance, which is really at the heart of the opposition.

Opponents argued that smoked marijuana is not a safe and effective medicine and that its approval would send the wrong message to young people.

More Bills in the 109th Congress

Bills have been introduced in recent Congresses to allow patients who appear to benefit from medical cannabis to use it in accordance with the various regulatory schemes that have been approved, since 1996, by the voters or legislatures of 13 states. This legislative activity continued in the 109th Congress.

Bills have been introduced in recent Congresses to allow patients who appear to benefit from medical cannabis to use it.

The States' Rights to Medical Marijuana Act would have transferred marijuana from Schedule I to Schedule II of the Controlled Substances Act. It also would have provided that, in states in which marijuana may legally be prescribed or recommended by a physician for medical use under state law, no provisions of the Controlled Substances Act or the Federal Food, Drug, and Cosmetic Act could prohibit or otherwise restrict a physician from prescribing or recommending marijuana for medical use, an individual from obtaining and using marijuana if prescribed or recommended by a physician for medical use, a pharmacy from obtaining and holding marijuana for such a prescription or recommendation, or an entity established by a state from producing and distributing marijuana for such a prescription or recommendation. Versions of this bill have been introduced in every Congress since the 105th in 1997 but have not seen action beyond the committee referral process.

Medical marijuana defendants in federal court are not permitted to introduce evidence showing that their marijuana-related activities were undertaken for a valid medical purpose under state law. The Steve McWilliams Truth in Trials Act would have amended the Controlled Substances Act to provide an affirmative defense for the medical use of marijuana in accordance with the laws of the various states. First introduced in the 108th Congress, this version of the bill was named for a Californian who took his own life while awaiting federal sentencing for marijuana trafficking. At his trial, the jurors were not informed that he was actually providing marijuana to seriously ill patients in San Diego in compliance with state law. The bill also would have limited the authority of federal agents to seize marijuana authorized for medical use under state law and would have provided for the retention and return of seized plants pending resolution of a case involving medical marijuana.

Neither bill saw action beyond the committee referral process. . . .

Medical Marijuana Patient Protection Act

In the second session of the 110th Congress, on April 17, 2008, Representative [Barney] Frank introduced H.R. 5842, the Medical Marijuana Patient Protection Act, to provide for the medical use of marijuana in accordance with the laws of the various states. Introduced with four original co-sponsors—Representatives [Sam] Farr, Hinchey, [Ron] Paul, and Rohrabacher—the bill would have moved marijuana from schedule I to schedule II of the CSA and would have, within states with medical marijuana programs, permitted

- a physician to prescribe or recommend marijuana for medical use;

- an authorized patient to obtain, possess, transport, manufacture, or use marijuana;

- an authorized individual to obtain, possess, transport, or manufacture marijuana for an authorized patient; and

- a pharmacy or other authorized entity to distribute medical marijuana to authorized patients.

No provision of the Controlled Substances Act or the Federal Food, Drug, and Cosmetic Act would have been allowed to prohibit or otherwise restrict these activities in states that have adopted medical marijuana programs. Also, the bill would not have affected any federal, state, or local law regulating or prohibiting smoking in public. In his introductory statement, Representative Frank said, "When doctors recommend the use of marijuana for their patients and states are willing to permit it, I think it's wrong for the federal government to subject either the doctors or the patients to criminal prosecution." Although differently worded, H.R. 5842 had the same intent as the States' Rights to Medical Marijuana Act, versions of which had been introduced in every Congress since the 105th in 1997. The bill was referred to the House Committee on Energy and Commerce and saw no further action.

Marijuana Possession and Use Should Be Decriminalized

Steven B. Duke

Steven B. Duke is professor of law at Yale Law School.

The drug-fueled murders and mayhem in Mexico bring to mind the Prohibition-era killings in Chicago. Although the Mexican violence dwarfs the bloodshed of the old bootleggers, both share a common motivation: profits. These are turf wars, fought between rival gangs trying to increase their share of the market for illegal drugs. Seventy-five years ago, we sensibly quelled the bootleggers' violence by repealing the prohibition of alcohol. The only long-term solution to the cartel-related murders in Mexico is to legalize the other illegal drugs we overlooked when we repealed Prohibition in 1933.

Mexico in Crisis

In 2000, the Mexican government disturbed a hornets' nest when it began arresting and prosecuting major distributors of marijuana, cocaine, heroin and amphetamines. Previously, the cartels had relied largely on bribery and corruption to maintain their peaceful co-existence with the Mexican government. Once this *pax Mexicana* ended, however, they began to fight not only the government but among themselves. The ensuing violence has claimed the lives of at least 10,000 in Mexico since 2005, and the carnage has even spilled north to the United States and south to Central and South America.

Some say that this killing spree—about 400 murders a month currently—threatens the survival of the Mexican government. Whether or not that is the exaggeration that Mexican President Felipe Calderón insists it is, Mexico is in crisis. The Mexicans have asked the [Barack] Obama administration

Steven B. Duke, "Drugs: To Legalize or Not," *Wall Street Journal*, April 25, 2009, p. W1. Reproduced by permission.

for help, and the president has obliged, offering material support and praising the integrity and courage of the Mexican government in taking on the cartels.

The U.S. should enforce its laws against murder and other atrocious crimes and we should cooperate with Mexican authorities in helping them arrest and prosecute drug traffickers hiding out here. But what more can and should we do?

The U.S. should enforce its laws against murder and . . . cooperate with Mexican authorities in helping them arrest and prosecute drug traffickers hiding out here.

Gun Control and Interdiction

Is gun control the answer? President Calderón asserts that the cartels get most of their guns from the U.S. We could virtually disarm the cartels, he implies, if we made it harder to buy guns here and smuggle them into Mexico. President Obama has bought into this claim and has made noises about reducing the availability of guns. However, even if the Obama administration were able to circumvent the political and constitutional impediments to restricting Americans' access to handguns, the effect on Mexican drug violence would be negligible. The cartels are heavily armed now, and handguns wear out very slowly.

Even if the Mexican gangsters lost their American supply line, they would probably not feel the loss for years. And when they did, they would simply turn to other suppliers. There is a world-wide black market in military weapons. If the Mexicans could not buy pistols and rifles, they might buy more bazookas, machine guns and bombs from the black market, thus escalating the violence.

Also hopeless is the notion—now believed by almost no one—that we can keep the drugs from coming into this country and thereby cut off the traffickers' major market. If we could effectively interdict smuggling through any of our 300-plus official border crossing points across the country and if we eventually build that fence along our entire border with Mexico—1,933 miles long—experience strongly suggests that the smugglers will get through it or over it. If not, they will tunnel under or fly over it. And there is always our 12,383 miles of virtually unguarded coastline.

The American Demand for Drugs

Several proposals have been submitted in the Mexican congress to decriminalize illegal drugs. One was even passed in 2006 but, under pressure from the U.S., President Vicente Fox refused to sign it. The proposals rest on the notion that by eliminating the profit from illegal drug distribution, the cartels will die from the dearth of profits. A major weakness in such proposals, however, is that the main source of the cartels' profits is not Mexican but American. Mexican drug consumption is a mere trickle compared to the river that flows north. However laudable, proposals to decriminalize drugs in Mexico would have little impact on the current drug warfare.

Secretary of State Hillary Clinton recognized the heart of the matter when she told the Mexicans last month [March 2009] that the "insatiable demand for illegal drugs" in the U.S. is fueling the Mexican drug wars. Without that demand, there would be few illegal drug traffickers in Mexico.

Once we have recognized this root cause, we have few options. We can try to eliminate demand, we can attack the suppliers or we can attempt a combination of both. Thus far, the Obama administration, like every other U.S. administration since drug prohibition went into effect in 1914, seems bent on trying to defeat the drug traffickers militarily. Hopefully, President Obama will soon realize, if he does not already, that this approach will not work.

Suppose the U.S. were to "bail out" the Mexican government with tens of billions of dollars, including the provision of military personnel, expertise and equipment in an all-out concerted attack on the drug traffickers. After first escalating, the level of cartel-related violence would ultimately subside. Thousands more lives would be lost in the process, but Mexico could thereby be made less hospitable to the traffickers, as other areas, such as Colombia, Peru and Panama, were made less hospitable in the past. That, after all, is how the Mexicans got their start in the grisly business. Eventually, the traffic would simply move to another country in Latin America or in the Caribbean and the entire process would begin anew. This push-down, pop-up effect has been demonstrated time and again in efforts to curb black markets. It produces an illusion of success, but only an illusion.

Marijuana Legalization and Regulation

An administration really open to "change" would consider a long-term solution to the problem—ending the market for illegal drugs by eliminating their illegality. We cannot destroy the appetite for psychotropic drugs. Both animals and humans have an innate desire for the altered consciousness obtainable through drugs. What we can and should do is eliminate the black market for the drugs by regulating and taxing them as we do our two most harmful recreational drugs, tobacco and alcohol.

An administration really open to "change" would consider a long-term solution to the problem—ending the market for illegal drugs by eliminating their illegality.

Marijuana presents the strongest case for this approach. According to some estimates, marijuana comprises about 70% of the illegal product distributed by the Mexican cartels. Marijuana will grow anywhere. If the threat of criminal prosecution and forfeitures did not deter American marijuana farmers, America's entire supply of that drug would be home-grown. If we taxed the marijuana agribusiness at rates similar to that for tobacco and alcohol, we would raise about $10 billion in taxes per year and would save another $10 billion we now spend on law enforcement and imprisoning marijuana users and distributors.

Even with popular support, legalizing and regulating the distribution of marijuana in the U.S. would be neither easy nor quick. While imposing its prohibitionist will on the rest of the world for nearly a century, the U.S. has created a network of treaties and international agreements requiring drug prohibition. Those agreements would have to be revised. A sensible intermediate step would be to decriminalize the possession and use of marijuana and to exercise benign neglect of American marijuana growers. Doing both would puncture the market for imports from Mexico and elsewhere and would eliminate much of the profit that fuels the internecine warfare in Mexico.

The health benefits and the myriad social and economic advantages of substituting regulation of hard drugs for their prohibition deserves serious consideration.

Decriminalizing Hard Drugs

After we reap the rewards from decriminalizing marijuana, we should move on to hard drugs. This will encounter strong resistance. Marijuana is a relatively safe drug. No one has ever died from a marijuana overdose nor has anyone gone on a violent rampage as a result of a marijuana high. Cocaine, heroin and amphetamines, on the other hand, can be highly addictive and harmful, both physically and psychologically. But prohibition makes those dangers worse, unleashing on vulnerable users chemicals of unknown content and potency, and deterring addicts from seeking help with their dependency. There is burgeoning recognition, in the U.S. and elsewhere, that the health benefits and the myriad social and economic advantages of substituting regulation of hard drugs for their prohibition deserves serious consideration.

A most impressive experiment has been underway in Portugal since 2001, when that country decriminalized the possession and personal use of all psychotropic drugs. According to a study just published by the Cato Institute, "judged by virtually every metric," the Portuguese decriminalization "has been a resounding success." Contrary to the prognostications of prohibitionists, the numbers of Portuguese drug users has not increased since decriminalization. Indeed, the percentage of the population who has ever used these drugs is lower in Portugal than virtually anywhere else in the European Union and is far below the percentage of users in the U.S. One explanation for this startling fact is that decriminalization has both freed up funds for drug treatment and, by lifting the threat of criminal charges, encouraged drug abusers to seek that treatment.

We can try to deal with the Mexican murderers as we first dealt with [Prohibition-era gangster] Al Capone and his minions, or we can apply the lessons we learned from alcohol prohibition and finish dismantling the destructive prohibition experiment. We should begin by decriminalizing marijuana now.

Marijuana Is Less Harmful than Alcohol

Steve Fox

Steve Fox is the director of state campaigns for the Marijuana Policy Project, an organization working to reform U.S. marijuana laws. He is coauthor of Marijuana Is Safer: So Why Are We Driving People to Drink?

Professor David Nutt didn't play the game. As the chief drug policy advisor in the British Government, an unspoken part of his job description was to help maintain a public fiction about marijuana—or cannabis, as it is known in the U.K. [United Kingdom] and other parts of the world. Specifically, he was expected to further the misperception of cannabis as a substance worthy of being classified and prohibited in a manner similar to more dangerous drugs like heroin and cocaine.

The Anti-cannabis Mythology

He made a big mistake at the end of last month [July 2009]. In a lecture at King's College in London, he spoke honestly—and truthfully—about the fact that cannabis is less harmful than alcohol and urged the government to factor the relative harms of substances into their policy-making. Moreover, he accused the British government of ignoring the evidence about the true harms of cannabis in order to reclassify the drug and increase penalties for possession.

Reacting with the logic and reason of a pub patron after last call, Home Secretary Alan Johnson immediately demanded that Prof. Nutt resign as the head of the Advisory Council on the Misuse of Drugs. He said Prof. Nutt had "crossed the line between offering advice and . . . campaigning against the government on political decisions."

More accurately, Prof. Nutt crossed the line between deceiving citizens and being honest with them. The home secretary, a former member of Parliament, is no doubt comfortable with a little verbal jousting over public policy decisions. What he could not abide by was a top ranking official threatening the anti-cannabis mythology embraced at the very top level of government. Based on Nutt's fateful bout of truthfulness, Johnson said he had "lost confidence" in Nutt as an advisor.

In a letter to Professor Nutt, Mr. Johnson explained how the system is supposed to work. He said: "As Home Secretary it is for me to make decisions, having received advice from the [Council] . . . It is important that the Government's messages on drugs are clear and as an adviser you do nothing to undermine the public understanding of them . . . I am afraid the manner in which you have acted runs contrary to your responsibilities."

[Anti-cannabis mythology] is all part of the game the government plays in order to maintain marijuana prohibition.

The Home Secretary's chief medical officer Sir Liam Donaldson put a similar spin on this hostile reaction to fact-based statements to the public. "These things are best sorted out behind the scenes," he said, "so that the government and their advisers can go to the public with a united front."

In the real world, what this means is that advisors are free to provide research or reports based on an honest assessment of the scientific evidence, but when this research is completely ignored in setting policy, they are expected to keep their mouths shut and move on as if nothing ever happened.

Ignoring Advice on Marijuana

This is all part of the game the government plays in order to maintain marijuana prohibition. In the United States, there are many examples of significant advisory opinions related to marijuana being completely ignored—even where the opinions were part of a decision-making process that should have led to action by the federal government.

In 1970, Congress established the National Commission on Marijuana and Drug Abuse to study marijuana and make recommendations about how to control its use. The Commission's final report suggested removal of criminal penalties, noting, "The actual and potential harm of use of the drug is not great enough to justify intrusion by the criminal law into private behavior." President [Richard] Nixon ignored the Commission's findings and launched and all-out war on marijuana users.

In 1988, Francis Young, an administrative law judge at the Drug Enforcement Administration (DEA), following hearings to determine whether marijuana should be placed into a less restrictive category under the Controlled Substances Act, wrote that marijuana should be moved from Schedule I (the most restrictive category) to Schedule II and it would be "unreasonable, arbitrary and capricious" to conclude otherwise. More than 20 years later, marijuana remains a Schedule I drug.

As recently as February 2007, an administrative law judge at the DEA issued an opinion concluding that it would be in the public interest for the agency to grant a license to the University of Massachusetts to grow a limited amount of marijuana to be used to study its potential therapeutic benefits. Faced with this seemingly rational opinion, the political powers at the DEA sat on it for nearly two years and then rejected it by formally denying the University the license in the very last days of the [George W.] Bush administration.

Myths About Marijuana

Of course, ignoring fact- and evidence-based advice about marijuana is just one part of the game our government has played over the past four decades. It has also gone out of its way to promote and spread myths about the drug—from the "gateway" theory to marijuana's supposed connection to cancer to the notion that "potent pot" is somehow more dangerous than "your father's marijuana." Each one has been debunked or proven wrong or misleading, but there is no doubt that they have helped keep marijuana illegal.

Yet there is one myth more insidious than the rest. And it is one that is as devastating as it is subtle.

You see, whether intentional or not, the government's greatest achievement when it comes to keeping marijuana illegal has been its ability to convince a majority of Americans that marijuana is as harmful as, if not more harmful than, alcohol. By doing so, it has secured alcohol's place as the recreational substance of choice for the vast majority of the public.

Influenced by the government's anti-marijuana propaganda, a large segment of our population is comfortable with a system that bans the use of marijuana but allows—and even celebrates—the use of alcohol, despite the fact that alcohol is objectively far more harmful.

The Harms of Alcohol and Marijuana

Let's consider just a few facts about the two substances. For starters, alcohol is far more toxic than marijuana. Just ten times the effective dose of alcohol can be fatal. Yet there has never been a recorded marijuana overdose death in history. The highly toxic nature of alcohol is also what leads to the all-too-frequent occurrences of nausea and vomiting from overindulgence.

Over the long-term, alcohol consumption is also far more likely to lead to the death of the user. According to the U.S.

Centers for Disease Control, between 33,000 and 35,000 Americans die annually from the effects of alcohol. The comparable number for marijuana? Zero. The supposed cancer-causing properties of marijuana? Non-existent.

Perhaps most disturbingly, as almost anyone who has been exposed to the two substances could tell you, alcohol is far more likely to produce dangerous and socially destructive behavior. It is cited as a contributing factor in 25–30 percent of violent crimes in this country and in about 100,000 sexual assaults on college campuses annually. These kinds of negative associations simply don't exist with marijuana.

Neither propaganda nor policy should be used to steer adults—or teens, for that matter—toward alcohol instead of marijuana.

Honesty About Marijuana

As mentioned at the beginning, facts like this were quite familiar to Professor Nutt. Even after his firing, he endeavored to spread the truth about the relative harms of marijuana and alcohol and urged parents to be especially wary of the one that posed the greatest potential for damage.

"The greatest concern to parents," he said "should be that their children do not get completely off their heads with alcohol because it can kill them . . . and it leads them to do things which are very dangerous, such as to kill themselves or others in cars, get into fights, get raped, and engage in other activities which they regret subsequently. My view is that, if you want to reduce the harm to society from drugs, alcohol is the drug to target at present."

Our nation's leaders might think this is a game, but it isn't. There are children and adults seriously suffering and even dying because of alcohol, and it is time our leaders started being honest and realistic about how it compares to marijuana—both in terms of public education and public policies. Neither propaganda nor policy should be used to steer adults—or teens, for that matter—toward alcohol instead of marijuana. This does not mean that marijuana is harmless; it simply means, and all of the evidence indicates, that it is less harmful than alcohol.

And no one should be fired for saying that.

The Prohibition on Marijuana Detracts from Real Drug Problems

Katherine Walkenhorst

Katherine Walkenhorst is a policy associate for Citizens Against Government Waste, a nonpartisan, nonprofit organization that works to eliminate waste, mismanagement, and inefficiency in the federal government.

As the Office of National Drug Control Policy (ONDCP), established in 1988 by the Anti-Drug Abuse Act, approaches its eighteenth year of existence, it continues to demonstrate its inability to either achieve its core objectives or function efficiently. The fiscal 2007 budget summary for the ONDCP, providing $245 million for the National Drug Control Strategy, proves that this year will be business as usual for the federal government and the ONDCP.

Despite consistent failures in reaching its own goals, the ONDCP continues to fund its four primary programs: High-Intensity Drug Trafficking Areas (HIDTA), the Counterdrug Technology Assessment Center (CTAC), the Drug Free Communities Program, and the National Youth Anti-Drug Media Campaign. The most wasteful aspect of these programs continues to be the media campaign that was created to reduce the use of marijuana in the United States. Despite a lawsuit concerning the integrity of the ad agency, a government report detailing the failure of the campaign, and a study revealing that the ads provide a reverse effect, the federal government, using the federal appropriations system, has decided to throw another $120 million at the problem in fiscal year 2007, a $30 million decrease from fiscal year 2006.

Katherine Walkenhorst, "Through the Looking Glass: A CAGW Special Report: Wasted in the War on Drugs: Office of National Drug Control Policy's Wasted Efforts," Washington, DC: Citizens Against Government Waste, 2006. Copyright © Citizens Against Government Waste. Reproduced by permission.

As the ONDCP continues to run this wasteful program, it is becoming apparent that it is attacking the wrong target. Although numerous studies have revealed that marijuana does not serve as a gateway drug, it continues to be the primary focus of the federal government's war on drugs. As methamphetamine and cocaine use continue to grow in the United States, the government refuses to acknowledge that its current prevention techniques are ineffective and wasteful. . . .

Students that are exposed to the ONDCP media campaign are more likely to try marijuana than those that are not exposed.

Since it was created in 1998, the National Youth Anti-Drug Media Campaign has been a failure. According to the campaign's website, the purpose of the project is "to educate and enable youth to reject illegal drugs, especially marijuana and inhalants." However, numerous studies done by public and private organizations revealing the failure of the campaign and the unearthing of scandals have proven the media campaign to be an abysmal failure. For example, an assessment performed by the Program Assessment Rating Tool (PART), set up by the federal government to determine the success of federal programs, has found since 2003 that the Youth Anti-Drug Media Campaign has failed to demonstrate results. According to the program results section of the assessment, "the outcome data from the evaluation suggests little or no direct positive effect on youth behavior and attitude attributable to the Campaign to date. Perhaps some positive effect on parental attitudes/behavior but that has not yet translated into an effect on youth. . . ."

While the ONDCP is being scammed by private ad agencies, it decided to do a little scamming of its own. In 2003 the ONDCP came under fire shortly after releasing a series of ads during the Super Bowl. Running on one of the most important nights for ad campaigns, the ads inaccurately maintained that drug users were directly aiding terrorism and linked unwanted teenage pregnancy to marijuana smoking. Along with demonstrating a complete lack of ability to reform the war on drugs, the media campaign took a turn for the worse by lying to the viewers and destroying the possibility of credibility.

More advertising misdeeds were revealed in a report released by the Government Accountability Office (GAO) in January 2005. The GAO determined that the drug czar's office illegally spent $155,000 on a series of ad campaign segments distributed to local TV news stations before the 2004 Super Bowl. The content of these clips contained "pre-packaged" news stories that led the viewer to believe that the reporting was coming from an independent third party, the news station. However, the "reporting" was actually a voice over script created and released by the ONDCP. According to the GAO report, more than 22 million households viewed these clips without the knowledge that they were created by a government agency. The report states, "ONDCP's prepackaged news stories constituted covert propaganda in violation of publicity or propaganda prohibitions."

A number of government studies ranging from the GAO to the ONDCP itself have determined that the ad campaign has been ineffective in decreasing the use of drugs among teenagers. Those results have been confirmed by private sector research. David Murray, an assistant professor at the Annenberg School for Communication at the University of Pennsylvania, found that the strides taken in drug and alcohol reform have nothing to do with the ONDCP. In fact, the areas that are reforming the most are not even part of the ad campaign. In one interview, Murray noted, "We are getting great benefits, but we aren't sure we have anything to do with it. Tobacco and alcohol consumption have fallen among teens, but the ONDCP doesn't address smoking or alcohol."

A study released in March 2006 contains information that might help eliminate all support for the National Youth Anti-Drug Campaign. According to the Department of Psychology at Texas State University, students that are exposed to the ONDCP media campaign are more likely to try marijuana than those that are not exposed. In the study, 229 18- to 19-year-old U.S. college students were asked to complete a short survey meant to determine each individual's attitude toward marijuana.

After completing the survey, students were asked to watch a 15-minute science program that contained ads from the National Youth Anti-Drug Campaign or anti-tobacco ads. The students were then given another survey to determine their attitudes on marijuana. The views toward marijuana became less negative among the students that were presented with the ads from the ONDCP than the group that watched the anti-tobacco ads. According to the researchers, the students that watched the anti-marijuana commercials were more likely to try marijuana than the students that watched the anti-tobacco commercials. If the results of this study are accurate, the government has thrown more than $1 billion at a campaign that has only succeeded in increasing the number of teenage marijuana users.

The Real Enemy

As U.S. funding continues to pour into hurricane relief efforts, the war in Iraq, and the Drug War, it is absolutely necessary that Congress exercise fiscal restraint and appropriate resources to the highest priorities. Unfortunately, the federal government has become so obsessed with decreasing marijuana use that it is spending money unwisely.

In order to defend its obsessive anti-marijuana ad campaign, the ONDCP has consistently made claims that halting the use of marijuana is critical because the substance serves as a "gateway" to more dangerous drugs. However, the ad campaign can only ride the coattails of that argument for so long. A 2002 study by the Rand Drug Policy Research Center, an institution that does not favor the legalization or decriminalization of marijuana, found that marijuana does not serve as a gateway to the use of heroin or cocaine. One of the primary researchers, Andrew Morral, stated:

> If our model is right, it has significant policy implications. For example, it suggests that policies aimed at reducing or eliminating marijuana availability are unlikely to make any dent in the hard drug problem. When enforcement resources that could have been used against heroin and cocaine are instead used against marijuana, this could have the unintended effect of worsening heroin and cocaine use.

This conclusion has been supported by a number of other research groups, such as the Sociology Department at the State University of New York at Stony Brook and the National Institute of Medicine. However, the ONDCP and the federal government refuse to heed the results of these studies, and continue to put excessive pressure on decreasing the availability and use of marijuana. Meanwhile, the use of methamphetamines, cocaine, and heroin continues to grow.

Although the ONDCP has reported growth in the use of methamphetamines and cocaine, it continues to use its funding to send messages to teenagers about marijuana.

One of the most pervasive drug problems in the U.S. is abuse of methamphetamine. The manufacture of this drug is easy and it has proven to be highly addictive and dangerous. While marijuana use in teenagers remains the primary focus of the ONDCP's ad campaign, the methamphetamine problem has been growing. A DEA [Drug Enforcement Administration] report concluded that while the use of methamphetamines was once most prevalent in the western part of the U.S., it has spread to almost every major metropolitan area, excluding the Northeast. According to figures released by the ONDCP in 2004, 2.5 percent of 8th graders had experimented with the use of methamphetamines. By 2005, that number had grown to 3.1 percent.

According to Senate Majority Leader Bill Frist (R-Tenn.), methamphetamine use, not marijuana use, is the most dangerous drug problem the U.S. is currently facing. On May 15, 2006 the Majority Leader spoke out in favor of the establishment of National Methamphetamine Prevention Week, stating, "I am delighted the resolution was adopted. It is an important issue. This is our number one drug problem today. We made real progress earlier in the year addressing the methamphetamine epidemic that is occurring across the country. Much more needs to be done." If Congress is willing to take the necessary measures to put methamphetamine use at the top of the agenda, the ONDCP, the Department of Justice, and the DEA must be willing to follow suit.

Along with the increased use of methamphetamine, increased cocaine use and availability continues to be a significant problem. According to figures provided by the ONDCP, cocaine use among college students jumped from 5.4 percent to 6.6 percent from 2003 to 2004. Like methamphetamine, cocaine is a highly addictive substance. While the cocaine-use trend has fluctuated since the late 1980's, one pattern has remained stagnant. Due to the addictive nature of the substance, heavy users of cocaine ensure that cocaine production remains at an all-time high, as the average heavy user consumes eight times more than the average first time or light user.

According to a Rand Drug Policy Research Center study, the number of heavy users and consumption of cocaine continue to increase. If the government continues to throw its resources toward the halting of teenage marijuana use, use of these more potent drugs will continue to expand. . . .

The federal government and the ONDCP have chosen to ignore evidence suggesting that the methods being used in the war on drugs are not effective. Despite numerous controversies and a failing ad campaign, the government continues to pour millions of tax dollars into the program. Although the ONDCP has reported growth in the use of methamphetamines and cocaine, it continues to use its funding to send messages to teenagers about marijuana. Unfortunately, these messages had the reverse effect: creating a positive image of marijuana in teenagers and young adults.

Marijuana Should Be Legalized for Medical Use

National Organization for the Reform of Marijuana Laws

The National Organization for the Reform of Marijuana Laws (NORML) is an organization that supports the rights of all adults to use marijuana responsibly, whether for medicinal or personal purposes, and supports the repeal of marijuana prohibition.

Marijuana prohibition applies to everyone, including the sick and dying. Of all the negative consequences of prohibition, none is as tragic as the denial of medicinal cannabis to the tens of thousands of patients who could benefit from its therapeutic use.

Evidence for Marijuana's Medical Value

Written references to the use [of] marijuana as a medicine date back nearly 5,000 years. Western medicine embraced marijuana's medical properties in the mid-1800s, and by the beginning of the 20th century, physicians had published more than 100 papers in the Western medical literature recommending its use for a variety of disorders. Cannabis remained in the United States pharmacopoeia until 1941, removed only after Congress passed the Marihuana Tax Act, which severely hampered physicians from prescribing it. The American Medical Association (AMA) was one of the most vocal organizations to testify against the ban, arguing that it would deprive patients of a past, present and future medicine.

Modern research suggests that cannabis is a valuable aid in the treatment of a wide range of clinical applications. These include pain relief—particularly of neuropathic pain (pain from nerve damage)—nausea, spasticity, glaucoma, and movement disorders. Marijuana is also a powerful appetite stimulant, specifically for patients suffering from HIV, the AIDS wasting syndrome, or dementia. Emerging research suggests that marijuana's medicinal properties may protect the body against some types of malignant tumors and are neuroprotective.

Virtually every government-appointed commission to investigate marijuana's medical potential has issued favorable findings.

Currently, more than 60 U.S. and international health organizations—including the American Public Health Association, Health Canada and the Federation of American Scientists—support granting patients immediate legal access to medicinal marijuana under a physician's supervision. Several others, including the American Cancer Society and the American Medical Association support the facilitation of wide-scale, clinical research trials so that physicians may better assess cannabis' medical potential. In addition, a 1991 Harvard study found that 44 percent of oncologists had previously advised marijuana therapy to their patients. Fifty percent responded they would do so if marijuana was legal. A more recent national survey performed by researchers at Providence Rhode Island Hospital found that nearly half of physicians with opinions supported legalizing medical marijuana.

Favorable Commission Findings

Virtually every government-appointed commission to investigate marijuana's medical potential has issued favorable findings. These include the U.S. Institute of Medicine [IOM] in 1982, the Australian National Task Force on Cannabis in 1994, and the U.S. National Institutes of Health Workshop on Medical Marijuana in 1997.

More recently, Britain's House of Lords' Science and Technology Committee found in 1998 that the available evidence supported the legal use of medical cannabis. MPs [members of Parliament] determined: "The government should allow doctors to prescribe cannabis for medical use. . . . Cannabis can be effective in some patients to relieve symptoms of multiple sclerosis, and against certain forms of pain. . . . This evidence is enough to justify a change in the law." The Committee reaffirmed their support in a March 2001 follow-up report criticizing Parliament for failing to legalize the drug.

U.S. investigators reached a similar conclusion in 1999. After conducting a nearly two-year review of the medical literature, investigators at the National Academy of Sciences, Institute of Medicine affirmed: "Scientific data indicate the potential therapeutic value of cannabinoid drugs . . . for pain relief, control of nausea and vomiting, and appetite stimulation. . . . Except for the harms associated with smoking, the adverse effects of marijuana use are within the range tolerated for other medications." Nevertheless, the authors noted cannabis inhalation "would be advantageous" in the treatment of some diseases, and that marijuana's short-term medical benefits outweigh any smoking-related harms for some patients. Predictably, federal authorities failed to act upon the IOM's recommendations, and instead have elected to continue their long-standing policy of denying marijuana's medical value.

Administrative Ruling Backs Medical Use

NORML [The National Organization for the Reform of Marijuana Laws] first raised this issue in 1972 in an administrative petition filed with the Drug Enforcement Administration [DEA]. NORML's petition called on the federal government to reclassify marijuana under the Controlled Substances Act as a Schedule II [from Schedule I, the most restrictive category] drug so that physicians could legally prescribe it. Federal authorities initially refused to accept the petition until mandated to do so by the US Court of Appeals in 1974, and then refused to properly process it until again ordered by the Court in 1982.

Fourteen years after NORML's initial petition in 1986, the DEA finally held public hearings on the issue before an administrative law judge. Two years later, Judge Francis Young ruled that the therapeutic use of marijuana was recognized by a respected minority of the medical community, and that it met the standards of other legal medications. Young found: "Marijuana has been accepted as capable of relieving distress of great numbers of very ill people, and doing so with safety under medical supervision. It would be unreasonable, arbitrary and capricious for DEA to continue to stand between those sufferers and the benefits of this substance in light of the evidence in this record." Young recommended "the Administrator transfer marijuana from Schedule I to Schedule II, to make it available as a legal medicine."

DEA Administrator John Lawn rejected Young's determination, choosing instead to invoke a differing set of criteria than those used by Judge Young. The Court of Appeals allowed Lawn's reversal to stand, effectively continuing the federal ban on the medical use of marijuana by seriously ill patients. It is urgent that state legislatures and the federal government act to correct this injustice.

The American public clearly distinguishes between the medical use and the recreational use of marijuana, and a majority support legalizing medical use for seriously ill patients.

Public Support for Medical Marijuana

Since 1996, voters in thirteen states—Alaska, California, Colorado, Hawaii, Maine, Michigan, Montana, Nevada, New Mexico, Oregon, Rhode Island, Vermont and Washington—

have adopted initiatives exempting patients who use marijuana under a physician's supervision from state criminal penalties. These laws do not legalize marijuana or alter criminal penalties regarding the possession or cultivation of marijuana for recreational use. They merely provide a narrow exemption from state prosecution for defined patients who possess and use marijuana with their doctor's recommendation. Available evidence indicates that these laws are functioning as voters intended, and that reported abuses are minimal.

As the votes in these states suggest, the American public clearly distinguishes between the medical use and the recreational use of marijuana, and a majority support legalizing medical use for seriously ill patients. A March 2001 Pew Research Center poll reported that 73 percent of Americans support making marijuana legally available for doctors to prescribe, as did a 1999 Gallup poll. Similar support has been indicated in every other state and nationwide poll that has been conducted on the issue since 1995. Arguably, few other public policy issues share the unequivocal support of the American public as this one.

Medical Marijuana and the Supreme Court

The Supreme Court ruled on May 14, 2001 that federal law makes no exceptions for growing or distributing marijuana by third party organizations (so-called "cannabis buyers' cooperatives"), even if the goal is to help seriously ill patients using marijuana as a medicine. Nevertheless, the Court's decision fails to infringe upon the rights of individual patients to use medical cannabis under state law, or the ability of legislators to pass laws exempting such patients from criminal penalties. This fact was affirmed by Justices [John Paul] Stevens, [Ruth Bader] Ginsburg and [David] Souter, who wrote in a concurring opinion: "By passing Proposition 215, California voters have decided that seriously ill patients and their primary caregivers should be exempt from prosecution under state laws for cultivating and possessing marijuana. . . . This case does not call on the Court to deprive all such patients of the benefit of the necessity defense to federal prosecution when the case does not involve any such patients."

NORML filed an amicus curiae (friend of the court) brief in this case, and hoped the Court would protect California's patient-support efforts from federal prosecution. The sad result of this decision is that tens of thousands of seriously ill patients who use marijuana to relieve their pain and suffering no longer have a safe and secure source for their medical marijuana. NORML calls on our elected officials to correct this injustice and is currently lobbying Congress to legalize marijuana as a medicine.

Marijuana Should Not Be Legalized

The Christian Science Monitor

The Christian Science Monitor *is an international news organization that delivers news coverage via its Web site, a weekly newspaper, and newsletters.*

The American movement to legalize marijuana for regular use is on a roll. Or at least its backers say it is.

They point to California Gov. Arnold Schwarzenegger, who said in early May [2009] that it's now time to debate legalizing marijuana—though he's personally against it. Indeed, a legislative push is on in his state (and several others, such as Massachusetts and Nevada) to treat this "soft" drug like alcohol—to tax and regulate its sale, and set an age restriction on buyers.

Several recent polls show stepped-up public support for legalization. This means not only lifting restrictions on use ("decriminalization"), but also on supply—production and sales. The [Barack] Obama administration, meanwhile, says the US Drug Enforcement [Administration] will no longer raid dispensaries of medical marijuana—which is illegal under federal law—in states where it is legal.

The push toward full legalization is a well-organized, Internet-savvy campaign, generously funded by a few billionaires, including [Hungarian American businessman] George Soros. It's built on a decades-long, step-by-step effort in the states. Thirteen states have so far decriminalized marijuana use (generally, the punishment covers small amounts and involves a fine). And 13 states now allow for medical marijuana.

Paul Armentano, deputy director of the National Organization for the Reform of Marijuana Laws (NORML), recently told a *Monitor* reporter that three reasons account for the fresh momentum toward legalization: 1) the weak economy, which is forcing states to look for new revenue; 2) public concern over the violent drug war in Mexico; and 3) more experience with marijuana itself.

If there is to be a debate, let's look at these reasons, starting with experience with marijuana.

Emergency-room admissions where marijuana is the primary substance involved increased by 164 percent from 1995 to 2002.

The Harms of Marijuana

A harmless drug? Supporters of legalization often claim that no one has died of a pot overdose, and that it has beneficial effects in alleviating suffering from certain diseases.

True, marijuana cannot directly kill its user in the way that alcohol or a drug like heroin can. And activists claim that it may ease symptoms for certain patients—though it has not been endorsed by the major medical associations representing those patients, and the Food and Drug Administration disputes its value.

Rosalie Pacula, codirector of the Rand Drug Policy Research Center, poses this question: "If pot is relatively harmless, why are we seeing more than 100,000 hospitalizations a year" for marijuana use?

Emergency-room admissions where marijuana is the primary substance involved increased by 164 percent from 1995 to 2002—faster than for other drugs, according to the Drug Abuse Warning Network.

Research results over the past decade link frequent marijuana use to several serious mental health problems, with youth particularly at risk. And the British Lung Foundation finds that smoking three to four joints is the equivalent of 20 tobacco cigarettes.

While marijuana is not addictive in the way that a drug like crack-cocaine is, heavy use can lead to dependence— defined by the same criteria as for other drugs. About half of those who use pot daily become dependent for some period of time, writes Kevin Sabet, in the 2006 book, *Pot Politics*— and 1 in 10 people in the US who have ever used marijuana become dependent at some time (about the same rate as alcohol). Dr. Sabet was a drug policy adviser in the past two presidential administrations.

He adds that physicians in Britain and the Netherlands— both countries that have experience with relaxed marijuana laws—are seeing withdrawal symptoms among heavy marijuana users that are similar to those of cocaine and heroin addicts. This has been confirmed in the lab with monkeys.

Today's marijuana is also much more potent than in the hippie days of yesteryear. But that doesn't change what's always been known about even casual use of this drug: It distorts perception, reduces motor skills, and affects alertness. When combined with alcohol (not unusual), or even alone, it worsens the risk of traffic accidents.

Marijuana and Crime

NORML likes to point out that marijuana accounts for the majority of illicit drug traffic from Mexico. End the illicit trafficking, and you end the violence. But that volume gives a false impression of marijuana's role in crime and violence, says Jonathan Caulkins, a professor at Carnegie Mellon [University] and a drug-policy adviser in the US and Australia.

It's the dollars that count, and the big earners—cocaine, methamphetamine, heroin—play a much larger role in crime and violence. In recent years, Mexico has become a major cocaine route to the US. That's what's fanning the violence, according to Dr. Caulkins, so legalizing marijuana is unlikely to quiet Mexico's drug war.

Neither are America's prisons stuffed with users who happened to get caught with a few joints (if that were the case, a huge percentage of America's college students—an easy target—would be behind bars). Yes, there are upward of 700,000 arrests on marijuana charges each year, but that includes repeat arrests, and most of those apprehended don't go to jail. Those who do are usually large-scale offenders.

Only 0.7 percent of inmates in state and federal prisons are in for marijuana possession (0.3 percent counting first-time offenders only, according to a 2002 US Justice Department survey). In federal prisons, the median amount of marijuana for those convicted of possession is 115 pounds—156,000 marijuana cigarettes.

The Costs of Legalizing Marijuana

The California legalization bill proposes a $50/ounce tax on marijuana. The aim is to keep pot as close to the black-market price as possible while still generating an estimated $1.3 billion in income for this deficit-challenged state.

But the black market can easily undercut a $50 tax and shrink that expected revenue stream. Just look at the huge trade in illegal cigarettes in Canada to see how taxing can spur a black market (about 30 percent of tobacco bought in Canada is illegal).

Legalizing marijuana is bound to increase use simply because of availability.

A government could attempt to eliminate the black market altogether by making marijuana incredibly cheap (Dr. Pacula at the RAND Organization says today's black market price is about four times what it would be if pot were completely legalized). But then use would skyrocket and teens (though barred) could buy it with their lunch money.

Indeed, legalizing marijuana is bound to increase use simply because of availability. Legalization advocates say "not so" and point to the Netherlands and its legal marijuana "coffee shops." Indeed, after the Dutch de facto legalized the drug in 1976, use stayed about the same for adults and youth. But it took off after 1984, growing by 300 percent over the next decade or so. Experts attribute this to commercialization (sound like alcohol?), and also society's view of the drug as normal—which took a while to set in.

Now the Dutch are finding that normalization has its costs—increased dependence, more dealers of harder drugs, and a flood of rowdy "drug tourists" from other countries. The Dutch "example" should be renamed the Dutch "warning."

Parents must make clear that marijuana is not a harmless drug.

As America has learned with alcohol, taxes don't begin to cover the costs to society of destroyed families, lost productivity, and ruined lives—and regulators still have not succeeded in keeping alcohol from underage drinkers.

No one has figured out what the exact social costs of legalizing marijuana would be. But ephemeral taxes won't cover them—nor should society want to encourage easier access to a drug that can lead to dependency, has health risks, and reduces alertness, to name just a few of its negative outcomes.

Why legalize a third substance that produces ill effects, when the US has such a poor record in dealing with the two big "licits"—alcohol and tobacco?

The Role of Parents

Legalization backers say the country is at a tipping point, ready to make the final big leap. They hope that a new generation of politicians that has had experience with marijuana will be friendly to their cause.

But this new generation is also made up of parents. Do parents really want marijuana to become a normal part of society—and an expectation for their children?

Maybe parents thought they left peer pressure behind when they graduated from high school. But the push to legalize marijuana is like the peer pressure of the schoolyard. The arguments are perhaps timely, but they don't stand up, and parents must now stand up to them.

They must let lawmakers know that legalization is not OK, and they must carry this message to their children, too. Disapproval, along with information on risk, are the most important factors in discouraging marijuana and cocaine use among high school seniors, according to the University of Michigan's "Monitoring the Future" project on substance abuse.

Parents must make clear that marijuana is not a harmless drug—even if they personally may have emerged unscathed.

And they need to teach the life lesson that marijuana does not really solve personal challenges, be they stress, relationships, or discouragement.

In the same way, a search for joy and satisfaction in a drug is misplaced.

The far greater and lasting attraction is in a life rooted in moral and spiritual values—not in a haze, a daze, or a munchie-craze.

Today's youth are tomorrow's world problem solvers—and the ones most likely to be affected if marijuana is legalized. Future generations need to be clear thinkers. For their sakes, those who oppose legalizing marijuana must become vocal, well-funded, and mainstream—before it's too late.

Marijuana Should Not Be Legalized for Medical Use

Drug Free America Foundation

The Drug Free America Foundation is a nongovernmental organization committed to developing, promoting, and sustaining global strategies, policies, and laws that will reduce illegal drug use, drug addiction, and drug-related injuries and death.

The controversial topic of "medical marijuana" is surrounded with confusing and contradicting information. Drug Free America Foundation, Inc. (DFAF) has studied the issue thoroughly and is committed to providing the most accurate information based on scientific and medical evidence. DFAF does not believe that crude marijuana, however, can be used safely as medicine.

Marijuana as Medicine

Crude marijuana is considered a Schedule 1 drug, the most restrictive designation given by the Controlled Substances Act (CSA) that places all drugs regulated by federal law into one of five schedules. What this means is that marijuana:

- has a high potential for abuse;

- has no currently accepted medical use in treatment in the U.S.;

- lacks the accepted safety for use of the drug under medical supervision;

- cannot be prescribed by a doctor;

- is not sold in a pharmacy; and

- is in the same category as heroin, LSD and Ecstasy (MDMA).

Drug Free America Foundation, "Why Crude Marijuana Is Not Medicine," Reproduced by permission.

Crude marijuana has been rejected for medicinal use by many prominent national health organizations including the American Medical Association, National Multiple Sclerosis Society, American Glaucoma Society, American Academy of Ophthalmology, American Cancer Society, National Eye Institute, National Institute for Neurological Disorders and Stroke and most importantly the Federal Food and Drug Administration (FDA).

Crude marijuana has been rejected for medicinal use by many prominent national health organizations.

Medications should be determined through scientifically valid research and the well established FDA process—not by the desires of a small group of individuals or the public's vote. The FDA is tasked with determining what is deemed as medicine. That process has been carefully constructed over the past century to protect patient health and safety. All medications, particularly those containing controlled substances, should become available only after having satisfied the rigorous criteria of the FDA approval process. Patients and physicians have the right to insist that prescription medications satisfy modern medical standards for quality, safety and efficacy. Such medications must be standardized by composition and dose and administered in an appropriate and safe delivery system with a reproducible dose.

The Five-Part Test for Medical Use

In *Alliance for Cannabis Therapeutics v. DEA [Drug Enforcement Administration]* ... (1994), the United States District Court for the District of Columbia accepted the Drug Enforcement Administration's five-part test for determining whether a drug meets "currently accepted medical use." The test requires that:

1. the drug's chemistry must be known and reproducible;
2. there must be adequate safety studies;
3. there must be adequate and well-controlled studies proving efficacy;
4. the drug must be accepted by qualified experts; and
5. the scientific evidence must be widely available.

Applying these criteria to crude marijuana, the court found that the drug had no currently accepted medical use. Preclinical and clinical studies are necessary to provide physicians with adequate information to guide their prescribing decisions. It is quite possible that in the near future we can anticipate that cannabinoid products will undergo clinical trials for their approval, and some may reach the market. There is no reason why medications derived from the cannabis plant should be exempted from the FDA process.

It is difficult to administer safe, regulated doses of medicines in smoked form.

Smoked Marijuana and the Pill Alternative

A pill form of the active chemical in marijuana, dronabinol (trade name—Marinol) currently exists and can be helpful for the nausea associated with chemotherapy or the wasting disease that appears with AIDS. But, even dronabinol is typically a third tier medicine. According to John A. Benson, Jr., M.D. of the Institute of Medicine, research on other cannabinoids is underway, and some of these chemicals may one day prove to be useful medicines. However, he states: "While we see a future in the development of chemically defined cannabinoid drugs, we see little future in smoked marijuana as a medicine." No FDA-approved medications are smoked.

It is difficult to administer safe, regulated doses of medicines in smoked form. Furthermore, the harmful chemicals and carcinogens that are byproducts of smoking create entirely new health problems. The California Office of Environmental Health Hazard Assessment, after an extensive review of over 30 scientific papers, declared that marijuana smoke causes cancer. The respiratory difficulties associated with marijuana use preclude the inhaled route of administration as a medicine. Smoked marijuana is associated with higher concentrations of tar, carbon monoxide, and carcinogens than even cigarette smoke. Recent studies show the following destructive effects of marijuana use:

- Respiratory damage

- Cardiovascular damage—it can dramatically increase heart rate

- Reproductive damage in men and women

- Immunosuppression

- Paranoia

- Emotional disorders

- Increased risk of schizophrenia and other neuropsychiatric disorders

- Memory loss

- Loss of ability to concentrate

- Increased tolerance to intoxication

- Addiction

- Leads to much higher use of other illegal drugs

- Linked to more violent behavior

Research on Effective Therapies

Long ago, the scientific and medical community determined that mere anecdotal reports of efficacy are not sufficient to warrant distribution of a product to seriously ill patients.

Marijuana is intoxicating, so it's not surprising that sincere people report relief of their symptoms when they smoke it. They may be feeling better—but they are not actually getting better. They may even be getting worse due to the detrimental effects of marijuana.

Legalization advocates would have the public and policy makers incorrectly believe that marijuana is the only treatment alternative for masses of cancer sufferers who are going untreated for the nausea associated with chemotherapy, and for all those who suffer from glaucoma, multiple sclerosis [MS], and other ailments. However, numerous effective medications are currently available for these conditions. According to Dr. Eric Voth, a Fellow of the American College of Physicians, some alleged uses for marijuana are to treat the nausea associated with chemotherapy or to create appetite stimulation in persons with AIDS, but there are better and safer FDA approved medications available such as Reglan, Zofran, Decadron, Compazine. Another remotely documented benefit is with spasticity for MS sufferers, but there are also better medicines available such as Baclofen, Amrix, Flexeril, Clonazepam, Robaxin and Neurontin.

Drs. Eric Voth and Richard Schwartz, experts on marijuana, having extensively reviewed available therapies for chemotherapy-associated nausea, glaucoma, multiple sclerosis, and appetite stimulation, determined that no compelling need exists to make crude marijuana available as a medicine for physicians to prescribe. They concluded that the most appropriate direction for research is to investigate specific cannabinoids or synthetic analogs rather than pursuing the smoking of marijuana, echoing the conclusion of the Institute of Medicine.

Organizations to Contact

The editors have compiled the following list of organizations concerned with the issues debated in this book. The descriptions are derived from materials provided by the organizations. All have publications or information available for interested readers. The list was compiled on the date of publication of the present volume; the information provided here may change. Be aware that many organizations take several weeks or longer to respond to inquiries, so allow as much time as possible.

American Civil Liberties Union (ACLU)
125 Broad St., 18th Fl., New York, NY   10004
(212) 549-2500
e-mail: aclu@aclu.org
Web site: www.aclu.org

The ACLU is a national organization that works to defend Americans' civil rights guaranteed by the U.S. Constitution by providing legal defense, research, and education. The ACLU opposes the criminal prohibition of marijuana and the civil liberties violations that result from it. The ACLU Drug Law Reform Project engages in campaigns and submits briefs in relevant law cases, with literature about these campaigns and text of the briefs available at the ACLU Web site.

American Council for Drug Education (ACDE)
164 W. Seventy-fourth St., New York, NY   10023
(800) 488-3784 • fax: (212) 595-2553
e-mail: acde@phoenixhouse.org
Web site: www.acde.org

The American Council for Drug Education seeks to diminish substance abuse. It creates accessible materials on the most current scientific research to those seeking accurate, compelling information on drugs. ACDE has resources about drug and alcohol abuse for parents, youth, educators, prevention professionals, employers, health-care professionals, and other concerned community members, including fact sheets on numerous substances. ACDE is an affiliate of Phoenix House Foundation, the largest private nonprofit drug abuse service agency in the country.

Cato Institute
1000 Massachusetts Ave. NW, Washington, DC   20001-5403
(202) 842-0200 • fax: (202) 842-3490
e-mail: cato@cato.org
Web site: www.cato.org

The Cato Institute is a public policy research foundation dedicated to limiting the control of government and to protecting individual liberty. The institute strongly favors drug legalization. The institute publishes the *Cato Journal* three times a year and the *Cato Policy Report* bimonthly.

Drug Free America Foundation (DFAF)
5999 Central Ave., Ste. 301, Saint Petersburg, FL   33710
(727) 828-0211 • fax: (727) 828-0212
Web site: www.dfaf.org

DFAF is a drug prevention and policy organization committed to developing, promoting, and sustaining global strategies, policies, and laws that will reduce illegal drug use, drug addiction, drug-related injury, and death. It opposes efforts that would legalize, decriminalize, or promote illicit drugs. DFAF publishes several position statements available on its Web site, including "Student Drug Testing Is Part of the Solution."

Drug Policy Alliance
70 W. Thirty-sixth St., 16th Fl., New York, NY   10018
(212) 613-8020 • fax: (212) 613-8021
e-mail: nyc@drugpolicy.org
Web site: www.drugpolicy.org

The Drug Policy Alliance, an independent nonprofit organization created in 2000 when the Lindesmith Center merged with the Drug Policy Foundation, supports and publicizes alternatives to current U.S. policies on illegal drugs, including marijuana. The alliance sponsors Safety First, a drug education program that advocates the harm-reduction approach to curbing teen drug use. Its Web site contains recent news on drug policy and links to other resources. Among the alliance's recent publications is the booklet for parents *Safety First: A Reality-Based Approach to Teens and Drugs.*

Human Rights Watch (HRW)
350 Fifth Ave., 34th Fl., New York, NY 10118-3299
(212) 290-4700 • fax: (212) 736-1300
e-mail: hrwnyc@hrw.org
Web site: www.hrw.org

Human Rights Watch is dedicated to protecting the human rights of people around the world. It investigates human rights abuses, educates the public, and works to change policy and practice. Among HRW's numerous publications is the report "Targeting Blacks: Drug Law Enforcement and Race in the United States."

Marijuana Policy Project (MPP)
PO Box 77492, Capitol Hill, Washington, DC 20013
(202) 462-5747
e-mail: mpp@mpp.org
Web site: www.mpp.org

The Marijuana Policy Project works to further public policies that allow for responsible medical and nonmedical use of marijuana and that minimize the harms associated with marijuana consumption and the laws that manage its use. MPP works to increase public support for marijuana regulation, lobbies for marijuana policy reform at the state and federal levels, and to increase public awareness through speaking engagements, educational seminars, the mass media, and briefing papers.

National Center on Addiction and Substance Abuse at Columbia University (CASA)
633 Third Ave., 19th Fl., New York, NY   10017-6706
(212) 841-5200
Web site: www.casacolumbia.org

CASA is a private nonprofit organization that aims to inform Americans of the economic and social costs of substance abuse and its impact on their lives while also removing the stigma of substance abuse and replacing shame and despair with hope. The organization supports treatment as the best way to reduce chemical dependency. CASA publishes numerous reports and books, including *Women Under the Influence.*

National Institute on Drug Abuse (NIDA)
6001 Executive Blvd., Rm. 5213, MSC 9561
Bethesda, MD   20892-9561
(301) 443-6245
e-mail: information@nida.nih.gov
Web site: www.nida.nih.gov

NIDA supports and conducts research on drug abuse—including the yearly *Monitoring the Future Survey*—to improve addiction prevention, treatment, and policy efforts. It publishes the bimonthly *NIDA Notes* newsletter, the periodic *NIDA Capsules* fact sheets, and a catalog of research reports and public education materials, such as *Marijuana: Facts for Teens* and *Marijuana: Facts Parents Need to Know.*

National Organization for the Reform of Marijuana Laws (NORML)
1600 K St. NW, Ste. 501, Washington, DC   20006-2832
(202) 483-5500 • fax: (202) 483-0057
e-mail: norml@norml.org
Web site: www.norml.org

NORML's mission is to move public opinion to achieve the repeal of marijuana prohibition so that the responsible use of cannabis by adults is no longer subject to penalty. NORML serves as an informational resource on marijuana-related stories and lobbies state and federal legislators in support of reform legislation. NORML has numerous research and position papers available at its Web site, including *Rethinking the Consequences of Decriminalizing Marijuana.*

Office of National Drug Control Policy (ONDCP)
Drug Policy Information Clearinghouse
Rockville, MD   20849-6000
(800) 666-3332 • fax: (301) 519-5212
e-mail: ondcp@ncjrs.org
Web site: www.whitehousedrugpolicy.gov

ONDCP, a component of the Executive Office of the President, establishes policies, priorities, and objectives for the nation's drug control program. ONDCP works to reduce illicit drug use, manufacturing, and trafficking; drug-related crime and violence; and drug-related health consequences. ONDCP has numerous publications related to its mission, including *Marijuana Myths & Facts: The Truth Behind 10 Popular Misperceptions.*

Partnership for a Drug-Free America
405 Lexington Ave., Ste. 1601, New York, NY   10174
(212) 922-1560 • fax: (212) 922-1570
Web site: www.drugfree.org

The Partnership for a Drug-Free America is a nonprofit organization that unites parents, scientists, and communications professionals to help families raise healthy children. The Partnership for a Drug-Free America equips parents with ways to prevent their children from using drugs and alcohol, and to find help and treatment for family and friends in trouble. Their online resource center features interactive tools that translate the latest science and research on teen behavior, addiction, and treatment into tips and tools for parents.

Rand Corporation
1776 Main St., Santa Monica, CA   90401-3208
(310) 393-0411 • fax: (310) 393-4818
Web site: www.rand.org

The Rand Corporation is a nonprofit organization that conducts research on important and complicated social problems. Its Drug Policy Research Center conducts research to help community leaders and public officials develop more effective ways of dealing with drug problems. *DPRC Insights* is its regularly published electronic newsletter that focuses on major drug policy issues.

Bibliography

Books

Arthur Benavie	*Drugs: America's Holy War.* New York: Routledge, 2009.
Richard Glen Boire and Kevin Feeney	*Medical Marijuana Law.* Berkeley, CA: Ronin, 2006.
Joseph A. Califano Jr.	*How to Raise a Drug-Free Kid: The Straight Dope for Parents.* New York: Simon & Schuster, 2009.
Mitch Earlywine	*Pot Politics: Marijuana and the Costs of Prohibition.* New York: Oxford University Press, 2007.
Vanda Felbab-Brown	*Shooting Up: Counterinsurgency and the War on Drugs.* Washington, DC: Brookings Institution Press, 2010.
Gary L. Fisher	*Rethinking Our War on Drugs: Candid Talk About Controversial Issues.* Westport, CT: Praeger, 2006.
Steve Fox, Paul Armentano, and Mason Tvert	*Marijuana Is Safer: So Why Are We Driving People to Drink?* White River Junction, VT: Chelsea Green, 2009.
Rudolph J. Gerber	*Legalizing Marijuana: Drug Policy Reform and Prohibition Politics.* Westport, CT: Praeger, 2008.

Hamid Ghodse, ed.	*International Drug Control in the 21st Century*. Burlington, VT: Ashgate, 2008.
Ryan Grim	*This Is Your Country on Drugs: The Secret History of Getting High in America*. Hoboken, NJ: Wiley, 2009.
Doug Husak and Peter de Marneffe	*The Legalization of Drugs*. New York: Cambridge University Press, 2005.
Joseph W. Jacob	*Medical Uses of Marijuana*. Bloomington, IN: Trafford, 2009.
Cynthia Kuhn, Scott Swartzwelder, and Wilkie Wilson	*Buzzed: The Straight Facts About the Most Used and Abused Drugs from Alcohol to Ecstasy*. 3rd ed. New York: Norton, 2008.
Peggy J. Parks	*Drug Legalization*. San Diego: ReferencePoint Press, 2009.
Doris Marie Provine	*Unequal Under Law: Race in the War on Drugs*. Chicago: University of Chicago Press, 2007.
Arnold S. Trebach	*Fatal Distraction: The War on Drugs in the Age of Islamic Terror*. Bloomington, IN: Unlimited, 2006.

Periodicals

Paul Armentano	"Testing Students for Drugs Is Neither Solution nor Bargain," *Fort Wayne (IN) New Sentinel*, September 21, 2005.

Radley Balko   "Drug War Casualties Left Behind,"
                      Atlanta Journal-Constitution, October
                      6, 2006.

Doug Bandow   "Arrest Michael Phelps Now!"
                      National Review, February 6, 2009.

Joseph A.   "Should Drugs Be Decriminalised?
Califano Jr.   No," *BMJ* , November 10, 2007.

Ted Galen   "Drug Prohibition Is a Terrorist's
Carpenter   Best Friend," *National Post*, January
                      4, 2005.

Ken Dermota   "Snow Fall," *Atlantic*, July/August
                      2007.

Drug   "The DEA Position on Marijuana,"
Enforcement   U.S. Department of Justice, May
Administration   2006. www.justice.gov/dea.

Economist   "How to Stop the Drug Wars," March
                      7, 2009.

David M.   "Cannabis Use and Other Illicit Drug
Fergusson, Joseph   Use: Testing the Cannabis Gateway
M. Boden, and L.   Hypothesis," *Addiction*, April 2006.
John Horwood

Conor   "Legalize Drugs Now," *Daily Beast*,
Friedersdorf   October 23, 2009.
                      www.thedailybeast.com.

Sanjay Gupta   "Why I Would Vote No on Pot,"
                      Time, January 8, 2009.

Ronald T. Libby — "Treating Doctors as Drug Dealers: The DEA's War on Prescription Painkillers," *Cato Policy Analysis*, June 6, 2005.

Tim Lynch and Juan Carlos Hidalgo — "Get Serious About Decriminalizing Drugs; Others Are," *San Jose (CA) Mercury News*, September 29, 2009.

Bruce Mirken — "The Case for Medical Marijuana," *Forbes*, August 21, 2009.

Jeffrey A. Miron — "Legalize Drugs to Stop Violence," CNN, March 24, 2009. www.cnn.com.

Kathleen Parker — "Phelps Takes a Hit," *Washington Post*, February 4, 2009.

Marsha Rosenbaum — "DARE: The Never-Ending Folly," *Orange County (CA) Register*, April 14, 2005.

Debra J. Saunders — "The Failed War on Pot Users," *San Francisco Chronicle*, October 20, 2005.

Norm Stamper — "Let Those Dopers Be," *Los Angeles Times*, October 16, 2005.

John Stossel — "Legalize All Drugs," *Jewish World Review*, June 18, 2008.

Ray Warren — "Because Marijuana Eradication Policy Is Hopeless, Tax and Regulate Instead," *Los Angeles Daily Journal*, July 19, 2007.

Robert S. Weiner   "The War Is Not Lost," *Washington Post*, August 22, 2007.

Index